MW00607552

Mastering Materials, Bindings, & Finishes

ROCKPORT

Mastering Materials, Bindings, & Finishes

The Art of Creative Production

Catharine Fishel

GLOUCESTER MASSACHUSETTS

ROCKPORT PUBLISHERS

© 2007 by Rockport Publishers, Inc.

All rights reserved. No part of this book may be reproduced in any form without written permission of the copyright owners. All images in this book have been reproduced with the knowledge and prior consent of the artists concerned, and no responsibility is accepted by producer, publisher, or printer for any infringement of copyright or otherwise, arising from the contents of this publication. Every effort has been made to ensure that credits accurately comply with information supplied. We apologize for any inaccuracies that may have occurred and will resolve inaccurate or missing information in a subsequent reprinting of the book.

First published in the United States of America by
Rockport Publishers, a member of Quayside Publishing Group
33 Commercial Street
Gloucester, Massachusetts 01930-5089
Telephone: (978) 282-9590
Fax: (978) 283-2742
www.rockpub.com

Library of Congress Cataloging-in-Publication Data
Fishel, Catharine M.
    Mastering materials, bindings, and finishes : the art of creative production / Catharine Fishel.
        p. cm. — (Design field guides)
    ISBN-13: 978-1-59253-324-4
    ISBN-10: 1-59253-324-8
    1. Commercial art—Technique. 2. Graphic arts—Technique. I. Title.
NC845.F57 2007
741.6—dc22   2006035856
                                                            CIP

ISBN-13: 978-1-59253-324-4
ISBN-10: 1-59253-324-8

10 9 8 7 6 5 4 3 2 1

Design: www.traffic-design.co.uk
Layout and Composition: Leslie Haimes

Printed in China

*Thank you to my real family
and to my Wood Badge family.
Your many kindnesses are a
daily inspiration.*

Feel like a   Feel like a   million dollars
                              every day...

Contents

Introduction

One of my favorite cartoons shows two cavemen conversing in front of a stone wheel. The first caveman, hands on fur-loincloth-covered hips, is asking the second guy, who clearly just finished carving, "What else ya got?"

I've saved this little scrap of paper for more than two decades because it speaks so clearly of the experience of the designer— or the art director, or writer, or any creative person, for that matter. Too often, it's the client, hands on business-suit-covered hips, asking the designer, "What else ya got?" Other times, though, it's the creative doing the asking—of the printer, paper supplier, or whoever else he or she looks to for ideas and goods.

That's because, despite the profusion of supplies, processes, and tools available today for creating graphic designs, there really is a finite number of ways to actually get the job done. Ink goes onto paper. Paper is cut or folded. Nonpaper

ingredients are incorporated. But designers continue to push and remix the finite; the borders are constantly forced outward. Who says you can't print an invitation on drywall? There is absolutely no reason you can't sew paper, build a snowman out of office supplies, or create a business card using an engraving process normally reserved for circuit boards.

The key to any new stretch, though, is that it stops short of being gimmicky. It's easy to attract attention by being extreme and ridiculous; it's much more difficult to make intelligent, witty choices and create a design that is truly innovative.

That's what connects all of the designs in this book. Some are really quite quiet, but their conceptual power makes them worthy of consideration. Each is an example of a designer looking at a design process or material in a completely different way. Each causes the recipient to touch the piece again, turn it over, wonder how it was done—or, even better, smile.

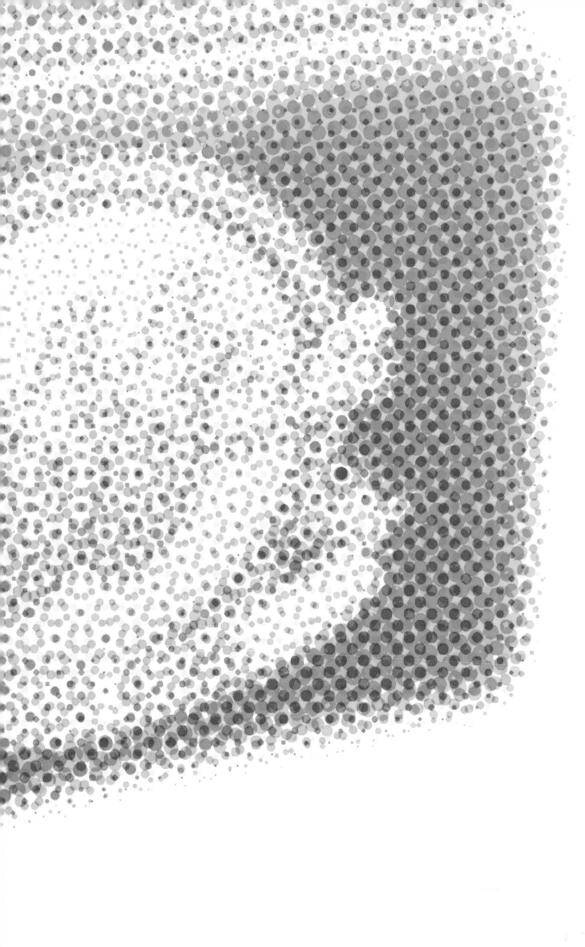

Chapter 1

Printing on Unconventional Surfaces:
Making the Medium the Message

Printing or imaging on an unconventional surface means committing wholeheartedly to feeding a specific concept: The substrate will (or should) say a lot about the concept behind the design. It's simply impossible to examine a design printed on metal, glass, cloth, plastic, or an unusual paper without wondering what's going on. The medium turns into a strong part of the message.

Almost anything a designer can lay his hands on can be imaged—even eggs and other edibles, if he uses food-safe inkjet printing. It's a matter of contacting the right vendor, explaining the project clearly, and understanding and recognizing the limitations of the surface. All designers and printers will agree that specifying an alternative printing surface is a challenge that requires special handling, forethought, additional cost, and, unquestionably, extra time in the schedule.

Another thing to keep in mind when specifying something other than good old paper is that the new substrate will not behave like paper. Processes such as scoring, trimming, punching, proofing, and even mailing won't proceed as usual. The application and drying time of ink will be different. Work with a specialist; it's worth the extra effort to search out a print provider with plenty of experience printing on materials you have in mind. Or, ask a trusted printer to try something new on press. He or she may welcome the challenge—a deviation from the everyday—and partner with you in unexpected ways for exceptional results.

Printing on Paper-Based Surfaces

Hundreds of paper-based or paper-related products are available for printing today, far too many to list in this section. Designers are repurposing products such as gift wrap, kraft paper, newsprint, artist's stock, security paper, and even wallpaper for their work, just to name a few examples.

It is crucial to provide the printer with a sample of an alternative stock before you commit to a final product. For instance, if offset printing is all the budget will allow, but won't work, the project will be compromised from the start. Create a back-up plan for how the designs might be trimmed from an alternative stock, as well. Rarely do these materials come in trim sizes that a standard litho press can handle. Dealing with excessive curl in the stock or waiting for extensive handling and special care on the drying end—all possibilities with alternative paper stocks— while on press will add to the budget.

Design Notes

> If they have the technology, some designers also print their work on alternate surfaces right in their own offices, as Bennett Holzworth of Be a Design Group did. He purchased several rolls of wallpaper for £0.5 per roll and screenprinted posters on the new "stock" himself. It took real work to fight the paper's inherent curl, and because of its thinness, he had to hand-trim the posters. The effort is worth it, he says, but only if the result is appropriate for the audience. (See page 23.)

"I would recommend doing something like this if you have an audience that might appreciate the hand-done qualities of the piece. I was trying to get the attention of designers with the posters, so something unusually produced was perfect," Holzworth explains.

Design Notes

> When Akiem Helmling of Underware Design specified Neobond for a book meant to be read in the sauna, he and his design team loved the synthetic paper's many excellent qualities, including its surface. (See page 22.)

Traditionally used for security and anticounterfeit documents, the paper printed well, was moisture resistant and durable, and could be manufactured with special fibers, chemically sensitive dyes, and positive watermarks. Helmling was surprised the paper was not specified more often by other designers. "A quick look at the bill made things more clear. Neobond is the real Rolls-Royce of paper," he says.

MORE ABOUT

Neobond Paper

Neobond is a durable synthetic fiber paper that can withstand almost any printing or production technique. Unlike some synthetic papers, it can be written on with pen or pencil. It is coated on two sides, which accounts, in part, for its higher cost.

The paper comes in a variety of colors and can be varnished, folded, perfed and drilled (with a few exceptions), glued, sewn, and even embossed. It can be printed with any conventional printing techniques except for rotogravure.

Its synthetic nature gives it high tear resistance as well as resistence to temperature extremes, moisture, and organic solvents. The manufacturer, FiberMark, can also add security features on manufacture so it can be used to prevent fraud.

tip

It's crucial to provide the printer with a sample of an alternate stock before a project begins. If offset printing won't work, for instance, and offset is all the budget allows, the project will be compromised from the start simply because of an unwise choice of substrate. Keep in mind how the designs will be trimmed out of an alternate stock as well; rarely do these materials come in trim sizes that a regular litho press can handle. Dealing with excessive curl in the stock or waiting for extensive handling and special care on the drying end of the press—all likely possibilities with alternate paper stocks— will add to the budget.

Printing on Plastic

Synthetics are an excellent choice for designers. Some are made for use on offset printing presses, but designers need not limit themselves to these; plenty of other plastic and even rubber surfaces can be imaged.

Almost any print process will produce images on synthetics, although care must be taken with the inks used; the wrong ink will never dry once laid on top of an impervious plastic surface. The main categories of plastic available for printing are listed here.

MORE ABOUT

Offset Printing

Offset printing, also called lithographic or photo-offset printing, is the most common commercial printing method in use today. With the process, an image is photographically or chemically imprinted on a printing plate; the image area is ink receptive, while the remainder of the plate is water receptive. The inked image is then transferred—or offset—from the plate onto a rubber blanket and then onto the paper or another substrate.

Types of Plastic Surfaces

Name	Durability	Characteristics	Uses
Polystyrene	one step up in durability from paper	resilient but very flexible	indoor or outdoor
Polyvinylchloride (PVC) or vinyl	one step up in durability from polystyrene	flexible or rigid	indoor or outdoor; flexible form can be used for static cling decals; rigid form is used in signage
Polyethylene	rigid and durable	flexible or rigid	indoor or outdoor; banners and signage
Polypropylene	UV-resistant; very durable	flexible	indoor or outdoor; menus, point of purchase, synthetic paper
Polycarbonate	very durable	flexible or rigid	often used for applications that require chemical resistance
Polyester	durable	flexible publication covers	overlays in books

When designing for printing on plastic or synthetic stock, keep the following points in mind. First, consider carefully what performance factors are needed in a design. Does it need to be flexible? foldable? waterproof? Need it be punched, die-cut, trimmed, folded, taped, glued, riveted, embossed, foil stamped, or endure any other finishing process? How much ink will be applied to the stock? What sort of drying time will this require?

The surface energy, or dyne level, of a plastic surface must fall between specific levels in order to print properly. If a dyne level is too low, the ink won't dry and will peel off. If it is too high, static problems will occur on press, and it will be difficult to get the plastic through the press. A printer experienced with running plastics has tests to help determine if a stock is suitable for printing.

Design Notes

> *Earl Gee and Fani Chung of Gee + Chung Design found out the hard way that printing on plastic can present unwelcome surprises. A cover design they had offset printed on polypropylene required five passes of opaque white before a red ink could be applied on top and remain true in color. (See page 24.)*

> *Then came a truly nasty surprise. "We were horrified to find that this slightly thinner weight of plastic curled back on itself a few hours after coming off press. The partial quantity of books that was delivered to our client curled back on itself a few hours after coming off press, and sitting on their cabinets began to curl like birds in flight," Earl Gee recalls. "The printer quickly did some tests and determined that simply varnishing the back side of the covers would put equal tension on the material and prevent it from curling."*

Static is also a problem when the job is off press, particularly with thin vinyls. Keep this in mind if a job calls for particular finishing processes after printing or if it requires more handling in your office.

Finally, scoring, trimming, or punching can be problematic if the punches, striking rules, or trimming knives are not angled properly or are not sharp enough. Plastic can crack, or ink can chip or fall off.

Static Electricity and Printing

Static electricity, as related to printing, is generally the printer's problem. Static buildup on press, a common dilemma, can cause foreign matter like dust to be attracted to print work, causing spoilage and slowdowns on press. Printers generally have devices installed to help control static.

Your client does not, however. After a job is printed, plastics can pose a real static problem, especially in cold or dry weather. A design that looked great in the controlled atmosphere of the printer's facility may start to stick to everything around it, including paper, other plastic, or even your hair and clothes.

Because you have no way of controlling the atmosphere, give any plastic you plan to print on a test-drive in the environment in which it must exist. Give it a week or so to acclimate before making your decision.

Design Notes

> *Because plastics are so versatile and are used in many industries, it can make sense to research other business lines for hints or resources. Designer Michael Schmalz of Refinery Design couldn't find the perfectly clear plastic he wanted to use for a business card for a stained glass business, so he eventually contacted a sign shop that used a liquid lamination process. This process not only provided the transparency he wanted but also made it impossible for his graphics to be scratched or rubbed off.*

> *"If you come up with a concept, there is a way to do it. Who would have thought of printing a business card at a sign shop? When you find the right producer, don't talk to the salesperson; talk to the person who runs the machines or who is in the art department. Especially in manufacturing environments, these people like to try something different and test the limits of their equipment," Schmalz says. (See page 39.)*

What Is a Dyne Level?

Dyne level measures the wetness of a surface. A scientist would say it is the measurement of the angle of the side of a drop of water sitting on the surface. When water beads on a surface, that substrate has a low dyne level. When water droplets flatten out, the surface has a high dyne level.

Dyne level is an indicator of how much surface energy the substrate has. The higher the dyne level, the more surface energy it has, and therefore the more receptive the surface is to accepting ink. Ink won't dry on or will peel off a surface whose dyne level is too low. An extremely high dyne level, on the other hand, can cause static electricity to build up on press.

Some plastics are manufactured for printing or can be specially treated so their surface dyne level is appropriate for printing. But some plastics simply will not accept ink well; consult an experienced printer before committing to an untried material.

MORE ABOUT

Liquid Lamination

Liquid lamination is an affordable way to protect a design, edge to edge, from some amount of abuse. These coatings physically protect a substrate from marring, handling, and moisture; in addition, some can provide UV light protection, thus preventing fading.

Liquid lamination also beefs up and enhances ink color and density. The coatings do not affect the flexibility of the printed design, and because the application is from edge to edge, the lamination keeps the substrate from peeling or falling apart. Some applica-tions can even be made over rivets so they become a secure part of a banner or sign.

Cost ranges from 5 to 20 cents per square foot (£ .03 to .10 per .09 sq meter). An experienced printer or signage professional can tell you where to obtain liquid lamination service.

reaction to the stresses placed on it by a press and devices such as gripper edges. Not only registration but proper placement of the printing on the substrate can be approximate at best.

Design Notes

> *Peter Kruty of Peter Kruty Editions discovered that special attention was definitely necessary when he decided to print an invitation on felt.*

"Working with felt presented some complex issues," says Kruty. "First, the felt arrived in a large roll and was hand-cut to run size. The felt sheets were singly fed into a Vandercook cylinder press and taped to the cylinder to avoid stretching the cloth. Normally, in this type of printing job, where we'd like consistently dense ink coverage, we like to double-drop the color on each sheet. But the felt's tendency to stretch and fall out of register forced us to run only one extrasaturated pass." (See page 36.)

MORE ABOUT

Gripper Edge

The gripper edge of a piece of paper, also called the feeding or leading edge, is the edge that leads through a printing press. This edge is held by the press's gripper fingers. Nothing can be printed in this area, which is usually $1/2$ inch (1.3 cm) to $3/8$ inch (1 cm) in depth.

tip

When paper is folded, it simply looks folded. When fabric is folded, especially for mailing, it may look wrinkled or unattractively creased. Consider carefully how the design will look once the recipient pulls it from the envelope.

Printing on Cloth

Screenprinting has long been the choice for printing on cloth, but today, digital printing offers another flexible choice. With a print resolution of 720 dpi and nearly limitless colors, digital can handle photographics, small type, fine lines, and designs that contain minute detail.

Cloth can be difficult to print on because it stretches, especially in

tip

If printing on metal proves impractical or cost-prohibitive, don't forget two easy options: labels applied to a metal surface or metallic inks or foil stamping printed on a nonmetallic surface.

Printing on Metal

Printing on metal is not a new idea: The first lithographic press, built in England around 1875, was actually designed to print on metal. Far more durable than paper, metal is a natural choice for projects that need to be weather safe, durable, and solid. Litho is one choice for printing, but acid etching, screenprinting, silkscreening, laser, and pad printing are also effective on metal. With an experienced printer's help, other print processes can be used as well. It's also possible to change the surface of metal with laser, chemical, or physical etching.

MORE ABOUT

What Is Silkscreening?

Silkscreening, or screenprinting, is a mechanical process. To produce an image, first, a screen (usually made of polyester or nylon, not silk) is stretched over a frame. Nonimaged areas are blocked off with stencil material; image areas are left open. The screen is placed over paper or another substrate; ink is placed at the top of the screen; and a squeegee is used to push an even layer of ink across the screen. The ink goes through the open areas of the screen, and when the screen is removed, the transferred image appears on the substrate.

Resolution of silkscreen graphics is determined by the mesh count of the screen and the absorbency of the substrate (the higher the mesh count, the higher the resolution). A mesh count of 230 delivers good results on a high-quality paper, while 110 or 160—ideal for printing on fabric—results in loss of detail on paper.

Metal Etching

Photochemical metal etching is a technique most often used to produce components for the electronics, medical, aerospace, and military industries, so it goes without saying that it is a highly accurate process. It is a low-cost way to transfer graphics onto flat metal or to produce new shapes. Metals from copper and stainless steel to exotic alloys can be processed.

Photolithography is used to transfer graphics onto metal by means of a photo-resist material. During etching with acid, the resist areas protects the image areas, and other sections are removed.

The advantages of etching over stamping, punching, and other processes that exert physical force on metal are that etching does not disturb the original properties or strength of metal, and no rough edges are left.

Metals to be etched must be quite thin. Any inside corners or turn tolerances in an etched line are directly proportional to the thickness of the metal. Ask a professional photochemical etcher to see samples of the company's work for ideas. Often, components produced for other industries have a wonderful graphical quality that may inspire your work.

Laser Engraving

Traditional engraving—with any sort of tool—exerts force, and therefore stress, on the surface of a substrate. Laser engraving does not. A beam of focused light, driven by a computer, cuts or otherwise burns and marks a surface to produce an image. This produces a crisp, permanent mark, and it is generally quicker—albeit more expensive—than traditional engraving.

Laser engraving is generally driven by a draw program. Its results are quite accurate and repeatable, but the process does have its limitations. For example, a traditional router is better able to carve away larger areas. Also, although resolution is quite good, the nature of the substrate—paper, metal, plastic, stone, wood, leather, rubber, or any other engravable material—determines final image quality and the time required to produce it.

What Is Pad Printing?

Pad printing is used for printing across small areas, particularly when they are neither nor difficult to reach. A thick, soft silicone pad picks up an inked image from a photo-etched plate and is then pressed directly against the item to be printed. The pad can wrap up to 180 degrees around the item. Only one color is applied at one time, but registration between passes is tight enough to permit four-color printing. Match colors can also be used. Light colors on dark usually require a double hit.

Pad printing is best for areas 1 inch (2.5 cm) in diameter or smaller. Also, large solid areas or small print sizes or line weights may be restricted by your printer. Check it out in advance before committing to a design.

The most important thing to keep in mind when designing for metal is that the substrate will likely not be raw metal—that is, it will probably have a coating that must accept ink well. Applied to protect the metal from scuffing, scratching, and other surface problems, coatings usually come in two types:

- **Thermoplastic:** After a thermoplastic coating is applied, it dries through evaporation or by moderate heat. Thermoplastic coatings are generally not resistant to high heat or solvents. If subjected to high heat as part of a print process, the coating is likely to melt. Exposed to chemicals used in some print processes (such as screenprinting), the coating may also be ruined.

- **Thermoset:** This type of coating is applied to the metal by baking it at high temperatures for long periods. Thermoset coatings are more resistant to heat, scuffing, and scratching.

  When specifying a metal surface, consult with an experienced printer as well as the metal supplier so that factors such as coating, weight, and trimming are discussed far ahead of time.

Inks such as those used in offset printing are transparent. When applied to metal, the metallic surface shows through, likely darkening the ink color and definitely throwing off the color cast. On solid metals or metallic foils, an underhit of opaque white is necessary if colors applied on top are to remain true. Also, each type of metal has a different color cast and a different degree of reflectivity; both of these factors affect final printed ink colors and the readability of applied graphics.

Printing on Wood or Leather

Wooden business cards have been around for years. In fact, a quick search of the Internet reveals a number of printers who specialize in imaging on wood of all types. Even if a wooden business card is not in the plans, these printers can be a good place to start when gathering information on the types of inks and wood to specify.

Silkscreening is the best choice for thicker surfaces, but veneers can be printed with offset. (Most tacky wood paneling is printed gravure, in fact.) Branding or burning also works.

Design Notes

> *For a wooden presentation folder, Creative Consumer Concepts—C3 used silkscreening. Art director Chris Evans says they were careful to select a silkscreening ink that would not require overdrying, which could affect the wood. For a self-promo project, the same company used laser etching to create wooden coasters.*

"Realize that each piece will accept the laser burning differently and will generate unique results," says Evans. This is perfect if a handmade effect is desired but not if exact replication is necessary. (See page 40.)

Leather is most often hot stamped. Hot stamping presses an image directly into the leather's surface. Foil stamping, branding, and even offset will work also, depending on the thickness of the leather. Again, search out leather manufacturers or companies that make things out of leather for advice on which varieties will print best and what print processes to use.

With both leather and wood, it's important to know if the substance is coated in any way or subjected to any other treatment, such as extreme heat or pressure.

MORE ABOUT

Gravure Printing

Like engraving, gravure printing is a form of recessed printing. Print rollers are engraved with a design. These recessed areas pick up a very fluid ink and deposit it on the surface to be printed. The process is frequently used for longer or frequent runs, such as for wallpaper. The process yields excellent fine details; as many as twelve colors can be accommodated on some presses. Both web- and sheet-fed printing are possible.

MORE ABOUT

Food-Safe Printing

Printing on food requires designers to consider carefully when selecting inks and production processes—and printing on food packaging requires almost as much care. In the United States, anything that comes into contact with food is regulated by the Food and Drug Administration (FDA), and other countries may have different restrictions.

Any image printed directly on food, generally through inkjet or laser application, is considered a food additive and strictly regulated. Approval for such printing must be obtained from the FDA. Printing that has indirect contact with food, such as on the outside of a package, also is restricted, but packaging manufacturers likely have all clearances and proper inks and processes already in place.

It's difficult to offer guidelines for designing for printing on food because, from chocolates to potato chips to eggs, each food surface is utterly different. The fat and moisture content of each food greatly affects its ink reception. In general, though, be aware that resolution is rarely high, and registration is almost always iffy. Color choices are almost unlimited, but multicolor printing is not recommended due to the difficulties with registration.

Printing on Transparent Surfaces

Glass and Plexiglas may seem unlikely substrates, but their transparency offers new depth to dimensions. Imaged areas offer one sort of effect, while the nonimaged areas, because they let light and the surroundings show through, provides the viewer with additional visual information.

For one-color—or actually no-color images—glass or Plexiglas can be etched chemically, mechanically, or by laser. The design is actually inscribed into the surface.

With a bit of care, it is also possible to put a multicolor image onto glass or Plexiglas with screenprinting, inkjet printing, or even offset lithography.

Design Notes

> *Oxide Design used the one-color, engraved option to produce a three-tiered promotion for its office. But getting the design just right took a lot of work.*

> *"Be prepared to go through a lot of research and development, trial and error. The more physical dimension the piece takes on, the more complex the process becomes to wrangle it into the precise form you're wanting," says creative director Rik Klingle-Watt. (See page 44.)*

Printing on Other Surfaces

When no printing process will work because the object being imaged is just too unconventional in shape, surface, or content—think golf ball—there are still options.

- Decals are a simple solution, but they involve a multistage process—printing on adhesive stock, followed by application—so costs are increased. Also, permanence can be a problem. Adhesive may also mar the surface to which it is applied, although many degrees of adhesion are available.

- Inkjet printing can be used on many surfaces and, depending on ink selection, can be anything from water-soluble to permanent. The trick is to find the right supplier. An experienced offset printer can probably point you in the right direction.

- The least familiar process to designers is likely to be pad printing. This technique is ideal for printing on surfaces that difficult to reach or are contoured. (See page 17 for more information.)

Design
Nassar Design

Creative director
Nélida Nassar

Designers
Nélida Nassar, Margarita Encomienda

Copywriter
Helen Goddard

Printer
Innerer Klang

Client
Nassar Design

Following 9/11, Nélida Nassar of Nassar Design wanted to send out a holiday message that was positive but not overpowering. She also wanted the design to transcend ethnic, religious, and national affiliations. So she specified a cracked ice paper usually used for gift wrapping, a gentle reminder of celebration. Letterpress printing was a must to make a solid impression on the paper's irregular surface without overpowering it.

Design
Ed Brodsky

Client
Lubell, Brodsky, Inc.

Lubell Brodsky used one-color offset printing on semitransparent artist's vellum to create an announcement that visually explained that the firm had moved to larger quarters, just around the corner.

Design
Underware

Akiem Helmling of Underware Design used an unusual ink on an unusual surface to create *Real Naked*, a book meant to be read in the sauna. The book is printed on Neobond, a synthetic fiber paper with built-in security features, which is normally used for secure documents such as passports, drivers' licenses, and stock certificates. It is impervious to moisture, so it is perfect for a sauna book. The design is offset printed with thermo-dynamic ink, which changes color, disappears, or reappears when subjected to temperature change—again, an excellent attribute for a sauna book.

Design
Be a Design Group

Art direction
Bennett Holzworth

Designer
Adrian Hanft

Client
Be a Design Group,
Nebraska AIGA

Bennett Holzworth of Be a
Design Group created two
designs with decidedly
unconventional printing
surfaces—old wallpaper and old
book covers—both items that
were already printed with
something else. The book
covers were fronts ripped from
old copies of *Reader's Digest*
picked up at garage sales; the
wallpaper was from a bin of
1970s rolls, just $1 (£0.5) each.
The book covers were
screenprinted and used as
postcards promoting the graphic
design book club of the
Nebraska chapter of the
American Institute of Graphic
Artists (AIGA). The wallpaper
posters were also silkscreened.

Design
Gee + Chung Design

Art director
Earl Gee

Designers
Earl Gee, Fani Chung

Illustrator
Earl Gee

Photographer
Geoffrey Nelson

Copywriter
David Chao (DCM)

Printer
Fong & Fong Printers and
Lithographer

The cover of this venture capital
offerings brochure was meant to
highlight the "clear differences"
that made this investment
opportunity attractive. So Earl
Gee of Gee + Chung Design
specified a transparent cover:
polypropylene with a matte
surface on both sides. The
design was offset printed on a
press equipped with a UV drying
unit, which sealed the ink onto
the plastic surface and helped it
dry faster. Offset printing ink is
transparent, so five passes of
white opaque ink were needed
for the red square on the cover
to cover the black square
underneath adequately. Printing
a clear varnish on the back side
of the material was required to
put equal tension on both sides
of the plastic to prevent curling.

Design
Kevin Akers Design + Imagery

Photographer
fogstock.com

Printing
Performance Printing Center

Designer Kevin Akers used
silkscreening to apply graphics
to a metal box that held an
oversized deck-of-cards-turned-
portfolio that he sends out to
promote his work. He used a
stock box and worked with a
promotional goods company to
get the printing done.

Design
Orlando Facioli Design

Production
Sediro Inoue

Client
Absolut Vodka

When Absolut Vodka launched Absolut Peach in sunny Rio de Janiero, it needed an invitation that could not be missed, by sight or by aroma. Orlando Facioli Design created a silkscreened beach bag that held an invitation and a box of real peaches. Whenever you print on anything other than paper, says the designer, plan a lot of extra time into the project. Using unusual printing surfaces is usually a new experience for everyone involved, so fully fleshed out comps are necessary.

Design
Studio Sägenvier
designkommunikation

Creative director
Sigi Ramoser

Copywriter
Hermann Brände

Type
Oliver Ruhm

Client
Lehrlings

Designer Sigi Ramoser used
branding for a client who
needed a rustic image to
accompany Johann the Trapper,
a promotional figure created to
encourage young people to stay
out of debt. Branding on wood
and other natural materials
was appro-priate given the
character's rustic nature.

Design
Creative Consumer
Concepts—C3

Creative director
Chris Evans

Designer, illustrator
Matt Loehrer

Client
Rubio's Fresh Mexican Grill

This wooden presentation folder
was screenprinted first, and then
its crosspieces were added; the
horizontal pieces would not have
allowed for proper screen
contact. Wood is absorbent, so
it's crucial to work with the
printer to select the right ink or
to add a coating to the wood
surface to restrict absorption.

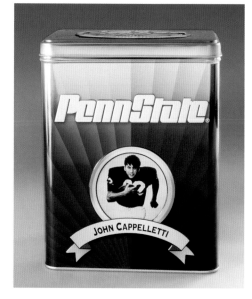

Design
Blockdot

Designer
Dan Ferguson

Marketing agency
The Sports Group

Client
Sunrise Coffee, Heisman
Winners Association

Blockdot Design specified tins
and foil bags, printing, and
stamp embossing to produce
this packaging featuring college
football's Heisman Trophy
winners. Spot white was laid
down first to keep certain colors
true, but in other areas the
metallic finish was allowed to
show through in order to create
a sense of electric energy and
excitement. The biggest
challenge for this project was
color matching, recalls designer
Dan Ferguson. "The tin material
was different from the bag
materials. Trying to find color
mixes that matched, using two
different materials, was tough.
You have to test, test, test,"
he says.

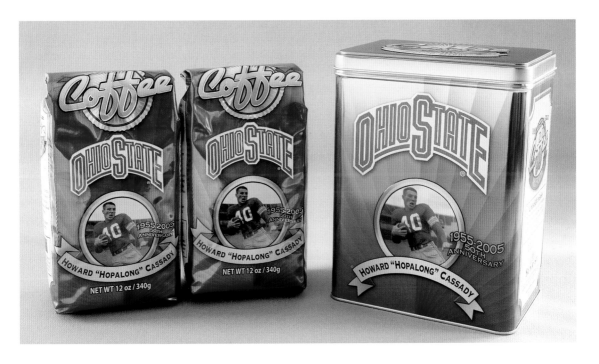

Design
Fossil

Designers
Patrick Reeves, John Dorcas

These tins borrow from the look and feel of matchbook art of the 1940s, the dull shine of their metal surfaces adding to the illusion.

Designers

Tim Hale, Brian Delaney

Shaped tins, like these Fossil watch containers, are printed flat and then stamped into shape. "A calculation is required for the distortion of the graphics as the tin is stamped so that everything lines up," explains art director Tim Hale.

Designers

Tim Hale, Brad Bollinger, Eric Venegas, David Eden

Printing on metal allows the designer to play heavily on the authentic, as the Fossil watch tins tucked in and amongst the real cans demonstrate. The design printed on the cans begins to trick the viewer's brain, but the fabricated can seals the deal.

Design
Designframe

Creative director
Michael McGinn

Designer
Sharon Greph

Printing
Peter Kruty Editions

For an announcement for a
film premiere at the Guggenheim
Museum, designer Michael
McGinn and Peter Kruty
Editions specified recycled felt, a
renewable resource that
connected with the film's topic:
the Industrial Revolution.
Photopolymer letterpress
printing applied words to the
cloth using an oil-based
lithography ink. Silkscreening
could have been used, but Kruty
says that letterpress produced
printing that looked *in* the sheet,
not just *on* the sheet.

Design
Grapevine

Art director, designer
Karen M. Bartolomei

Calligraphy
Xandra Y. Zamora for
XYZInk.com

This save-the-date booklet,
part of an elaborate wedding
invitation, is covered with
brown Japanese silk glued to a
300 gsm cotton sheet to make it
stiff enough for engraving.
Designer Karen Bartolomei of
Grapevine says she chose
engraving on cloth to simulate
embroidery, but it was difficult to
make the engraving ink stick to
the fabric. Registering two
colors was also difficult. With
any such printing challenge,
double the stock order to
allow for spoilage, the
designer says.

Design
Creative Consumer
Concepts—C3

Creative director
Chris Evans

Associate art director
Ed Schlittenhardt

Creative Consumer Concepts—
C3 designed screenprinted
rubber binders for Panda
Express, a gourmet Chinese
restaurant. When screenprinting
on rubber, says art director Chris
Evans, it's necessary to chemically remove the coating to allow
for adequate bonding of the ink.
Evans also had a clear coat
applied after printing to protect
the design from scratching.

Design
Refinery Design Company

Client
Archiglass

Designer Michael Schmalz thought the most compelling way to represent the work of Archiglass, a group of artisans who creates custom designs for architectural installations, was through a clear card that features the firm's work. After nine months' worth of research looking for a purely clear card, Schmalz finally went to a high-end sign company that uses a proprietary inkjet process to print on clear plastic. The ink is stable when exposed to the elements, and it is printed onto liquid lamination in reverse, then run through a heat process and melted onto a substrate. It is laminated onto another piece of plastic with just a bit of opaqueness and a different surface. The finished card has a smooth surface and a rougher surface; the ink is trapped inside so it does not rub off.

Design
Creative Consumer
Concepts—C3

Creative director
Chris Evans

Art director
Joy Merritt

Client
Creative Consumer
Concepts—C3

Part of a Creative Consumer
Concepts—C3 holiday party kit,
the branded coasters shown
here were laser-burned with the
company's logo. Each piece is
slightly different because the
grain of each piece of wood
varies and thus burns differently.

Design
Grapevine

Etching on Plexiglas requires special considerations. The designer for this invitation, Karen Bartolomei, says she kept the type size about 16 point. The engraving must be done slowly so the plastic does not bubble from the heat of the laser, so be sure to build plenty of time into the schedule, she says. Ask for a sample before committing to the entire job, and remember that the Plexiglas has depth, so be sure the shipping envelope can expand to accommodate its thickness.

Design
Oxide Design

Designers
Drew Davies, Joe Sparano

Photographer
Brycebridges.com

Client
Oxide Design

Glass was the substrate of choice for this Oxide Design promotion, for several reasons. Oxide designers wanted the design to make a tangible impression; this they achieved by sand and laser etching into the glass. Also, although glass is basically a one-color vehicle, it is transparent. The design was constructed so that when the pieces were stacked, they revealed a secret message: the company's logo.

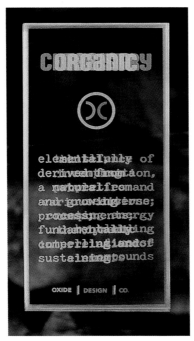

Design
Blu Concept, Inc.

Creative director
Rik Klingle-Watt

Designer
Lindsay Rankin

Copywriter
John Vigna

Printer
Glenmore Printing

A shopping center client was embarking on a massive eighteen-month construction project that would be announced at its annual general meeting. Designers at Blu Concept were challenged to create an invitation to the meeting that would not only spark the interest of what could be a jaded audience but also allude to the construction. The result: The client liked the mock-up so much, he wouldn't give it back. Traditional silkscreening was used for imaging, but it turned out to be a complicated process when the printer had to stop every few passes to clean the drywall dust out of the screen.

Design
Vrontikis Design Office

Art director
Petrula Vrontikis

Logo designer
Katsuhiko Nakamachi

Client
Global-Dining, Inc.

These chocolates, produced for
an elegant shop in Tokyo that
creates handmade candies,
were printed using a very simple
method: Before the surface of
the chocolate is firm, a transfer
sheet carrying the print is laid on
its surface, and edible ink is
applied. The only requirement is
that the imaged surface be
perfectly flat.

Chapter 2

Specialty Inks and Coatings

The ability to print on everything from paper and plastic to eggshells and drywall, as described in the previous chapter, is made possible largely by the enormous number of specialty inks and varnishes available today. With tools that range from liquid inks to dry toners, it's nearly impossible to find a surface exempt from imaging.

But even though designers use plenty of ink, they don't purchase it outright—so they are not likely to subscribe to the magazines or belong to the organizations printers do. So it's crucial to have a close working relationship with a knowledgeable printer when it comes to researching what inks and coatings are available, as well as how to get and use them. Sometimes, too, it may be necessary to search out print vendors in other industries, such as sign and textile manufacturers, to achieve specific results. Alternatively, go directly to the source—whoever makes or preps the substrate on which you want to work, whether it is plastic, wood, or metal. These people understand the chemical structure of the substrates to which more chemicals—inks, toners, or other coatings— will be added. Proper chemistry makes everything work.

Inks and Coatings

Here is a necessarily incomplete list of the inks and coatings available today:

Glitter/Metallic

Colors available: Silver or gold usually available off the shelf; other colors can be formulated on request

Opacity: Good

Standard print applications: All but silkscreening

Considerations for designers and printers:

- Ink in reservoir on press must be constantly agitated to prevent metal particles from settling.

- May require extra drying time.

- The best effects are achieved on smooth or coated papers.

- Unless topcoated with varnish, metallic inks may scuff or offset onto other items.

- Unless topcoated with varnish, metallic inks may tarnish over time and/or show fingerprints.

- Not ideal for outdoor applications or fabrics that will be washed.

- Excellent to prevent fraud/counterfeiting, as metal particles in the printed original photocopy or scan dark or even black.

Pearlescent

Colors available: A wide range of subtle pastels

Opacity: Transparent

Standard print applications: Flexography, rotogravure

Considerations for designers and printers:

- Can be printed over nonpearlescent colors to enhance sheen, almost like a varnish.

- Can be used alone to create subtle highlights.

- Ink contains a blend of mica and titanium dioxide, which causes color shifting at various angles and light sources.

- The best effects are achieved on smooth or coated papers.

- The coarser the product, the higher the degree of glitter and the more difficult to use on press.

Food-Safe

Colors available: All colors and additives are controlled by the Food and Drug Administration; consult experienced printer for advice.

Opacity: Extremely varied; depends on printing surface

Standard print applications: Pad printing, silkscreen, rotogravure

Considerations for designers and printers:

- There are three categories of food-safe inks: Those safe for use around foods (signage in a kitchen); those that may come in contact with food (labeling on food packaging); and those used directly on food.

- Safe inks are also available for medical settings (they are safe to be touched with latex gloves, for instance, or won't dissolve or bleed when in contact with alcohol or other chemicals).

MORE ABOUT

Predicting Special Effects

It can be tough enough for a designer to predict the exact effects of a process, spot or pricy specialty ink, varnish, or other coating on any paper stock. Trying to get a client to picture the shine or gloss or exact color is almost impossible.

A good solution is to try PrintDevisor software, from StoneCube (www.stonecube.com). It accurately displays—on screen—what is essentially the degree of light reflectivity for any number of surfaces combined with specialty coatings or special effects, such as foil stamping or embossing. (PrintDevisor 2 will also show die-cutting, sculpted embossing, and designs applied to common packaging shapes.) The company worked closely with Eckart, an international specialty ink and pigment manufacturer and supplier, to devise the exact algorithms to allow special effects to be viewed accurately on screen.

The program works with Adobe Creative Suite and QuarkXPress and is Mac and PC compatible.

Scented

Colors available: Clear overprint

Opacity: Transparent

Standard print applications: All

Considerations for designers and printers:

- Prints clear over graphics, like an overprint of varnish. Does not affect color below.

- Hundreds of scents are available, and with additional cost, new scents can be formulated.

- Lead times of two weeks or longer are required for new formulations.

- Lasting scent can be improved by multiple hits.

Glow-in-the-Dark

Colors available: Range from natural (green-emitting) to yellow, orange yellow, orange, rose, green, and blue

Opacity: Transparent to semi-opaque

Standard print applications: Flexography, silkscreen, offset, rotogravure

Considerations for designers and printers:

- Cost increases as glowing power and longevity increase.

- White undercoat may improve performance of phosphorescent layer.

Thermochromatic

Colors available: Many options in low-temperature, body-temperature, and high-temperature activation levels

Opacity: Room-temperature color changes at specified temperature activation levels to clear or lightly shaded color

Standard print applications: Flexography, silkscreen, offset

Considerations for designers and printers:

- Excellent choice to prevent counterfeiting.

- Cost is roughly ten times more than that of a normal printing ink.

- Can be treated like a spot color on press.

Photochromatic

Colors available: Wide range; usually, colors change from a light shade or clear to a true color when exposed to UV light

Opacity: Transparent until exposed to UV light

Standard print applications: Flexography, silkscreen, offset

Considerations for designers and printers:

- Excellent choice to prevent counterfeiting.

- Cost is roughly ten times more than that of a normal printing ink.

- Can be treated like a spot color on press.

While specialty coatings offer the designer plenty of creative options, it's important to remember that specifying them sometimes requires a leap of faith. The printer often does not have much experience with new materials, and seldom is there an equivalent to a Pantone swatch book for you to consult. This can be a challenge for a worried designer trying to predict results, but it will probably be even more of a jump for a client who can't even dream of what the final scratch-and-sniff, pearlescent, foil-stamped design will look like.

Design Notes

> *Renee Rech of Renee Rech Design says that testing ink through drawdowns is a must, especially with choices like glow-in-the-dark and heat-sensitive inks. "Test the transparency of the inks first to see what you are working with," she says. "We had some issues with the four-color printed images underneath showing through until we did multiple tests and found solutions to remedy it." (See page 52.)*

Foil Stamping

Foil stamping—also called foil blocking, hot stamping, foil imprinting, and leaf imprinting—uses a heated die strike to apply a colored, clear, metallic, matte, pearlescent, opalescent, marbled, shiny, holographic, or otherwise tinted foil to another surface. Foils can be opaque or semitransparent. The process can be combined with embossing for a dimensional effect; applied on top of flat printed graphics for a bit of shine or extra emphasis; or used alone to create its own effects.

Almost any image can be foil stamped, but the process does have its limits. The stamping process is a mechanical one—a heated die imposes the foil onto the printing surface—so registration can be off a bit from hit to hit. Type sizes should stay above 8 point, and lines should be no thinner than 2 points. Foils tend to fill in in tight areas, such as tightly kerned type or lines that are closely spaced, so reserve the effect for more open areas.

Smooth, coated stocks work best for foil stamping. Uncoated or textured surfaces present an irregular surface that may disrupt and break up the foil. However, large areas of stamping can bubble on highly coated stock if the chemistry between the two layers is not carefully considered. Also, foil stamping on top of coatings or inks with high wax levels will also cause the foil to adhere improperly. Aqueous and other wax-free coatings are best for using underneath foils; ask an experienced foil stamp supplier for guidance on getting the most effective results.

As with specialty inks, foils often do not survive the heated rigors of laser printers and high-speed copiers, so be conscious of the possible final uses of a design. Ask your printer for laser-safe resins instead. Also, some foils mark and scratch easily, especially in large, flat areas, so make sure clients are aware the stamped surface could become marred with use.

tip

Foils are great for any design that must be secure or should not be copied, as they produce an extra challenge for counterfeiters and usually disappear or appear black on copies.

tip

Tiny details such as serifs do not take foil well, although it is possible to hit an area twice.

Thermography

Thermography is another specialty treatment that can add shine or pizzazz to a design. Sometimes called poor man's engraving, the process produces raised images that are visible and tactile. Thermal powders are applied to wet ink and then heated. The powder melts into a solid mass, adhering to the printing surfaces and producing the raised image. Excess powder is suctioned off prior to heating.

Powders are available in transparent and opaque versions and in a variety of pastel, primary, and metallic colors. Finishes include dull, matte, semi-gloss, and gloss. The process has been used on stationery systems for years, but it can be used on any design—with a few limitations:

- Thermography can be done on one side of a sheet only.

- The effect should not be applied over folds, as the solid materials will crack.

- Type should be no smaller than 6 points, and faces that are particularly condensed or fine will fill in; the powders used for thermography are not fine enough to provide such tiny detail. Also, don't combine large, flat areas with fine elements, as the particle sizes needed—either coarse or fine—will not work for one or the other.

- Large, flat areas of thermography may appear mottled or bubbled. Consider applying the effect to finer lines, such as on a grid, or smaller features in a design, to greater dramatic effect.

- Avoid bleeding thermography, as trimming can cause it to crack.

Good Advice for Good Results

Almost all specialty inks cost more than conventional inks. Some take longer to dry, so extra time and money must be built into the project. The degree of coating on paper can also affect drying time: Highly glossy papers take longer to cure and dry, although the effect of specialty ink— particularly metallic and pearlescent inks—is more pronounced on coated paper.

Keep in mind that not all specialty inks and coating are safe for use with lasers or copiers. High temperatures can melt all of those great graphics that cost extra on press. Also, finishing processes such as punching, trimming, and folding—as well as other processes that involve heat—can crack, flake, or otherwise ruin a specialty treatment. Be sure to check with the printer and even the ink manufacturer before disaster strikes.

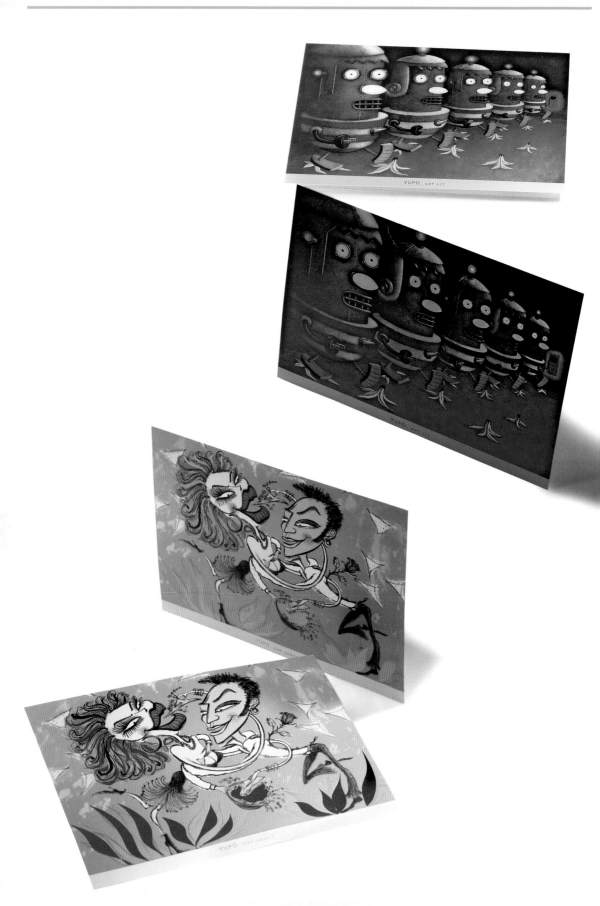

Design
Renee Rech Design

Designer
Renee Rech

Illustrators
Richard Borge, Cathy
Gendron, Keith Graves,
Joe Sorren, Katherine
Streeter, YUCEL

Client
Yupo Corporation

This postcard campaign
featured specialty inks and
effects—including glow-in-the-
dark and heat-sensitive inks,
as well as lenticular foils,
embossing, and die-cutting
—on different cards. The
specialty inks were applied
over four-color printed images,
which could have resulted in
unexpected show-through in
some spots, had the issue not
been addressed in advance.
It is crucial, Rech says, to do
drawdowns and tests with such
inks before a project begins.

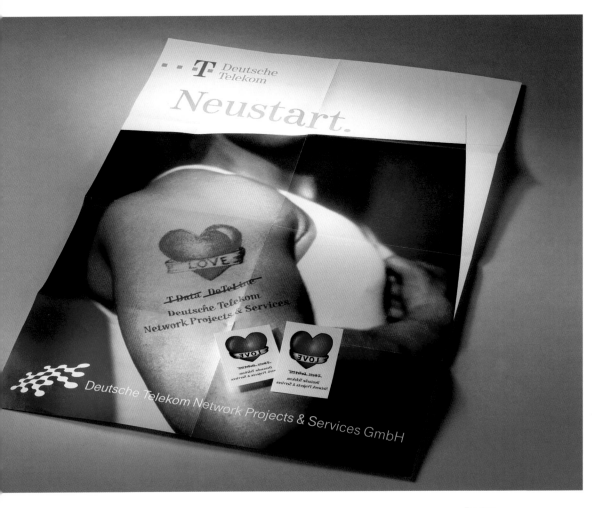

Design
Stereobloc, Berlin

When the two daughter companies of Deutsche Telekom, T-Data and DeTeLine, were merged in the Deutsche Telekom Network Projects and Services, the process was rational, complex, and economical. But for the newly combined staffs, it was also highly emotional. To help address the emotional level, Stereobloc designers created a temporary tattoo and accompanying poster that put the merger on a more personal, humorous level, says designer Holger Stumpe. The poster was a regular offset print job, but a printer who specializes in this sort of work created the tattoo. Finding the tattoo printer was a challenge, says Stumpe, but the actual printing of the tattoo was easy and not especially costly, with normal art prep.

◄ **Design**
Rule29

Art direction
Justin Ahrens

Designers
Justin Ahrens, Dan
Hassenpleg

Printer
O'Neil Printing

Photographer
Brian MacDonald

Rule29 designer Justin Ahrens
was looking for "cheesy" ideas
for a holiday card when he
thought of the ubiquitous pine
tree air freshener. His design
used a rub-and-smell varnish on
top of four-color stochastic
printing, plus a drilled hole and
hanger to complete the effect.
Ahrens says he could also have
used a scented aqueous
silkscreen coating to create the
aroma or even a scented paper.
But he says the varnish, which
added about 20 percent in cost
to the project, has the longest
shelf life.

➤ **Designer**
Tomato Kosir

Copywriter
Tomato Kosir

Printer
Grafex

For the eighth Slovenian Film
Festival, an event that takes
place mostly at night, when a
majority of printed materials are
not visible to a film audience,
designer Tomato Kosir decided
to create a poster and catalog
design that would be. He
combined two major concepts
of the festival—motion and
light—in a blurred design that
uses glow-in-the-dark ink. The
effect was well worth the
additional cost, he says, which
was about twice as much as
regular inks.

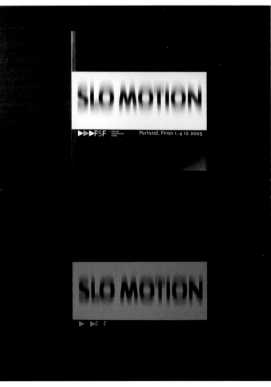

Design
Nassar Design

Creative director, artist
Nélida Nassar

Designers
Nélida Nassar, Nadine Nassar

Copywriter
Nathan Kerman

Photographer
Tom Powel Imaging, Inc.

Printer
Merrill Daniels

Client
Sperone Westwater Gallery

This catalog is a compilation of Nabil Nahas's last show, titled "Opium and Candy," which featured large, highly textured work. The paintings are made from acrylic mixed with pumice. To replicate this effect, designer Nélida Nassar of Nassar Design mixed textured pumice beads into silkscreening ink for the printing of the black dots on the catalog cover. The challenge, says Nassar, was to select a proper screen mesh that would allow the beads to pass through at the proper density with clogging, as well as to find a way to stack and store the books so they did not scratch each other. The printer solved the first difficulty, and a clear, curable UV coating solved the second.

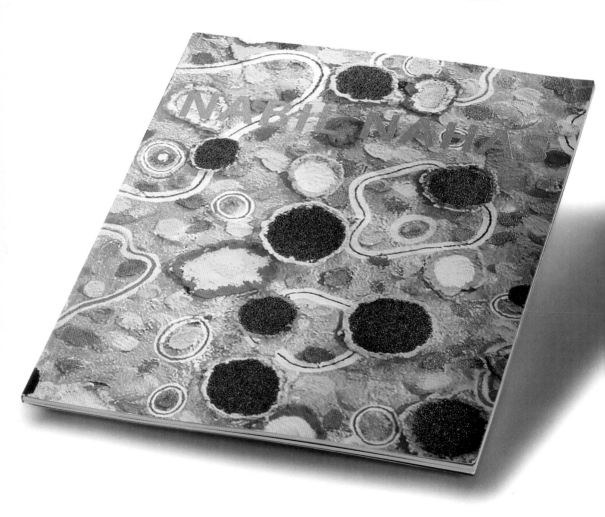

Design
Iggesund Paperboard

Production
Pomco

Photographer
Gyrotour and Reverso Septant
Platin from Jaeger-LeCoultre,
Switzerland

The incredible sculpted quality
of these printed images makes
them look as though they were
real, three-dimensional objects.
The effect was created by
printing four-color on top of
multilevel embossed foil areas
enhanced with spot UV and
spot gloss coatings.

Design
Sussner Design Company

Art director
Derek Sussner

Designer
Brandon Van Liere

Copywriter
Jeff Mueller, Floating Head

Printer
Reflections

Client
Reflections

Sometimes subtlety is the best approach to addressing a design problem. For a printer client called Reflections, the designers as Sussner Design Company used registered embosses and debosses and a clear foil-stamped effect to create the barest reflection of the company's new identity. Designer Brandon Van Liere says that maintaining register was tough. "If you plan on embossing or debossing, pay particular attention to the typeface you pick. In our case, the letters in Reflections appear much thinner when embossed, and normal or slightly thicker when debossed," he says.

Design
Form

Art direction, design
Paul Benson, Nick Hard

Client
Caro

Form Design repurposed a part of a client Caro's identity program—repeat patterns—in a holiday card. The designers used a textured die and foil stamping to create the effect. The shine is enhanced by the angles introduced to the foil by the texture, creating a festive look.

Design
Form

Art direction
Paul West, Paula Benson

Designers
Claire Warner, Nick Hard

Client
Granite

The pressure applied during foil stamping creates the slight impression of debossing on this card design, created by Form. The gunmetal gray stamp is a wonderful compliment to the duplex stock, with orange on one side and gray on the other. When duplexing stock for any project, Form designer Tom Hutchings says, make sure the grain of the two paper stocks goes in opposite directions so the sandwiched stocks won't start to bow.

Design
Ruth Huimerind, Syri Loun

Photographer
Ruth Huimerind

Paper skirt (not shown)
Krista Leesi

Copywriter
Peeter Sauter

Printer
K-Print

Client
Modo Paper

Modo, a wholesale company that sells paper products, asked Ruth Huimerind to create a Christmas card that showcased some of its products. Huimerind took advantage of the client's specialty products, even foil stamping on tissue paper. "It's extremely unhandy to stamp on tissue paper," says the designer, "so if somebody does it for you, you must be grateful."

Design
Ruth Huimerind, Syri Loun

Copywriter
Peeter Sauter

Printer
Aktaprint

Client
Sampo Bank

Designer Ruth Huimerind
encouraged her client, a
conservative bank, to move
toward a more creative design
for a recent Christmas card.
She combined foil stamping
on an exclusive pearlescent
French paper called Evanescent
with die-cutting on a card stock
insert inside to create a starlike
effect that literally shines. Testing
the foil stamping on the stock
beforehand ensured that the job
would print well, she says.

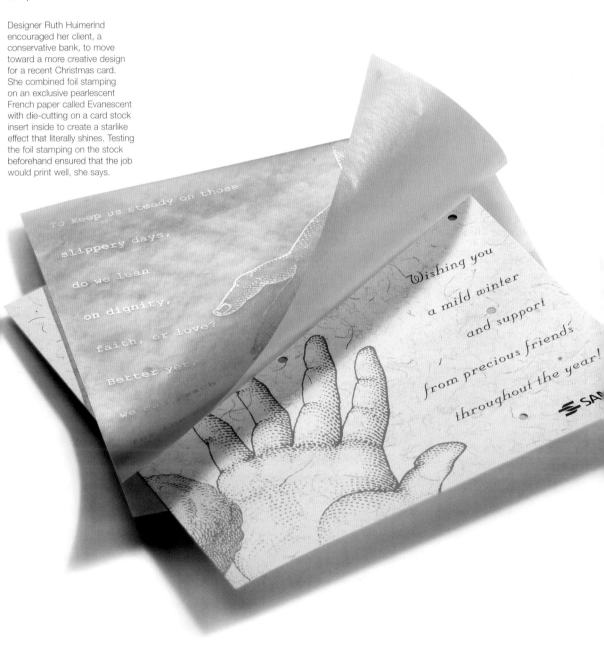

Design
Hollis Brand Communications

Designers
Don Hollis, Angela Villarreal

For a minimalist, modern coastal hotel, Hollis Brand Communications designed an open and airy guest room directory that visually described the facility's architecture. The modular in-room services menu was tilted upright in a glasslike plastic container that was hot foil-stamped.

Design
Boccalatte

Flocking
Flock Finishers

Printer
Peachy Print

Flocking is a process that is nearly extinct, but the design firm Boccalatte felt it was perfect for an invitation to an event for seniors. It established a sense of nostalgia through the eyes and the fingertips. The process is surprisingly simple, says Boccolatte's Cheri Cunningham: The base is spot-glued where flocking is desired, then put through a machine that sets fibers onto the stock. Make sure any paper stock specified for this process is thick, adds Cunningham, and have a decent schedule and budget.

Chapter 3

Unique Bindings: Fasteners and Closures

The notion that books and other multisheet or multipart compilations should be bound is so strong that even the Internet—the technology that promised to do away with paper documents—is built from websites that have a common binding convention: a cover sheet or home page that holds everything together. It seems our brains want things to be organized and fastened together.

Binding is a practical and oftentimes necessary component of a design, and it also plays an important conceptual role. This is a lesson that designers learn well and early. Student designers are often charged with binding an assignment or creating an extremely short-run project, and the binding is almost always a major part of the concept. The trick—post school—is to be able to use the same creative approach on much longer runs and to accomplish the task on budget and on time.

Alternative Materials

Working with alternate materials in binding requires special considerations. Metal bindings or covers were likely machined prior to arrival on the bindery floor, so special handling or milling may be required to eliminate sharp edges. A special cord used in a hand-binding application may initially feel strong, but the die-cut holes through which it is laced may saw at and eventually cut through the cord. Any deviation from standard binding methods should be considered from a worst-case standpoint in order to forestall disasters. After all, it's one thing if a varnish isn't shiny enough; it's quite another if a design actually falls apart in the client's hands.

Design Notes

> *Designer Orlando Facioli combined plastic spiral binding with a heavy metal cover for a fashion book. "This project had to be planned in advance because when you are not working on an ordinary paper project, everything takes more time. You need to get everything approved in advance. Also, never do anything without getting a model approved first," he says.*

Design Notes

> *Close coordination with a reliable printer and binder is essential: Pensare Design's Amy Billingham says that when she and her team began designing their own split-page, Wire-o–bound calendar, they weren't sure it was technically possible to accomplish what they wanted. Pensare relied heavily on its printer for guidance on setting up files, selecting paper, and so on. In the end, the project took ten rather than the hoped-for six weeks, but Billingham feels it was a success.*

> *Her advice for such projects, especially those that are time-sensitive: "Start designing early."*

Binding Options

It would be nearly impossible to build an exhaustive list of all of the creative binding options available. Hundreds of designers are likely dreaming up even newer and more creative ones at this very moment. That being said, the possibilities generally fall into one of three categories:

Machine Binding

This category includes traditional binding methods, such as perfect binding, saddle-stitched binding, and other bookbinding standbys. Other possibilities include older and sometimes forgotten techniques, such as case binding. A quick search of the Internet reveals hundreds of ideas and binderies.

Combination Machine and Hand Assembly

This category includes binding methods that take advantage of automated finishing processes, such as folding and drilling. The latter is especially flexible, as a set of drilled holes can be threaded through with connectors as varied as nuts and bolts, leather thong, string or cord, ribbon, rubber bands, or just about anything else flexible and long enough to be used as a tie. These methods combine some amount of machined production with a certain degree of handwork.

Hand Assembly

The final category includes binding techniques that are achieved entirely by hand. Japanese bindings, hand-stitching, sewing machine stitching, and glued application of bindery elements are just a few examples. Although the results of such methods are generally eye-catching and distinctive, the processes by their nature require more time in the schedule, which often limits the print run.

Japanese Stab Binding

Laying a template with pre-punched holes on the edge of the booklet and securing it with clamps makes it easy to accurately punch holes in every cover and page so that they register perfectly.

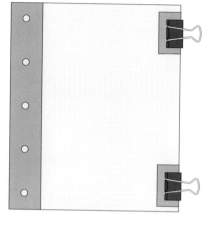

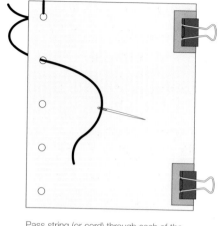

Pass string (or cord) through each of the holes in turn, securing the first stitch with a knot as shown. Once the string has gone through each hole, pass through each one again, this time in the other direction.

Finally, pass through each of the holes again, but this time, also pass a stitch around the outside edge of the pages. After the string has reached the bottom of the packet again, pass through all of the holes again, progressing to the top, and secure the string with another knot. The order of the stitches and their direction are not as important as their appearance in relationship to the design and effectiveness in fastening.

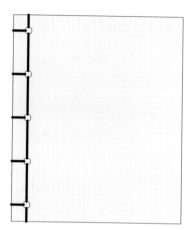

MORE ABOUT

Japanese Stab Binding

With this ancient binding style, a number of holes are drilled or stabbed through the left edge of numerous sheets of paper or covers that must be bound together. Then, a needle and thread is passed through the holes numerous times to complete a pattern that runs thread through each hole from top to bottom and also around its edge.

Perfect Binding

Perfect binding uses adhesive to hold signatures or single pages together on their edge. The technique yields a flat surface on the bound edge; it is relatively durable, but it is not ideal for designs that must lie flat. Most paperbacks, trade publications, and magazines are perfect bound. It is a less expensive bindery option than stitching or stapling.

Case Binding

A case-bound book is a specific kind of hardcover book created by gluing cover material to stiff boards that are, in turn, attached to the book's endsheets. It is the most common sort of binding used for textbooks.

MORE ABOUT

Saddle, Loop, and Side Stitching

Saddle stitching: A common binding option for booklets and magazines, saddle stitching binds multiple signatures by opening them at their center and stitching them together through their fold line. The name comes from the supports the folded sheets rest on, called *saddles*.

Loop stitching: A variation on saddle stitching in which the stitch (wire) is formed into a loop that sticks out beyond the spine of a book. The loops enable the piece to be slipped onto the rings of a three-ring binder.

Side stitching: Binding in which folded signatures or pages are stitched along the side near the gutter margin. Side-stitched designs do not lie flat.

Design Notes

> *Print runs can be limited even further by spoilage, which is a natural outcome of experimental binding methods. Take the case of the hand-bound snowman card featured in this chapter. Multiple processes meant more steps and therefore more places for things to go wrong.*
>
> *"There were many unusable cards in this project. The black paint on the rivets flaked off in some cases, getting on the rest of the cards. We had to examine each one and erase those areas with a white eraser," recalls designer Becky Gelder.*

Slipcases

A slipcase, essentially a heavy chipboard or otherwise rigid sleeve used to house usually printed components, is a smart choice in a number of situations. Not only does it protect its contents from dust, light, and other environmental effects but also it can hold together disparate or floppy components—say, CD cases and an accompanying book, a stack of magazines, loose sheets of paper, or a set of binders. A traditional slipcase is open on one end or side; the opening may also be covered with a lid or flap. Many slipcases are coated with printed paper, so print process can also be added to a design.

Keep these points in mind when designing a slipcase:

- The slipcase is necessarily taller than its contents. Make sure the design is not so tall that it won't fit on a bookcase.

- If the slipcase has an open end, take advantage of the exposed spines of the contents are and give them an interesting graphic treatment.

- A slipcase whose open edge is flush with its contents' edges should have half-moon cutouts in each side of the case so people can use their fingers and thumb to grasp and extract the contents easily.

Slipcases can be ordered from package manufacturers, but the Internet will yield many sources for slipcase-specific manufacturing.

Spiral Binding

Spiral binding uses a cylindrical spiral of metal or plastic to bind pages that have been specially punched on their edge. It's a good binding choice for any design that must lie flat. The spiral coils have bulk and can catch on each other, which may complicate storage and stacking. The spiral can also be crushed or otherwise bent or broken, compromising the binding. Also, unless a gatefolded front cover is designed to fold back on itself and around the spine to the back cover, there is no printable spine.

A variation of spiral binding is Wire-o binding, a series of parallel wire loops attached along a wire. This technique is stronger than a single spiral and tends to allow pages to be turned more easily.

Both spiral and Wire-o binding can accommodate covers made from alternate materials, such as metal, plastic, rubber, and even wood. Any layout created for spiral or Wire-o must include a generous binding (or gutter) margin to leave room for the required punches.

Design
Full Circle Marketing and Design

Creative director
Gregg Burns

Art director, designer
Andy Filius

Account executive
Todd Mellema

Photographer
Dean Vandis

Copywriter
Patrick Duncan

Client
Battle Creek Area Mathematics and Science Center

For a math and science center brochure, Full Circle Marketing and Design wanted to integrate science into every facet of the design. The designers also needed to find a way to keep the brochure contents from spilling, as the brochure was a series of cards rather than a bound piece. Magnets glued to the front and back covers held everything together, including the covers, while contributing to the overall concept. The magnets are nickel-plated circles with a holding force of 1 pound (.45 kg), so they are quite strong.

Design
Citizen Scholar

Designer
Randy J. Hunt

Client
Wheat Würtzburger, photographer

The cover of this photographer's portfolio is laser-printed on an adhesive 3M reflective Mylar that was then mounted to book board. The Mylar is so strong it actually serves as the hinge for the book. A fixative was applied primarily to protect the laser toner, but designer Randy Hunt discovered it also diffused the Mylar's shine to a silky softness while the color stayed bright—a happy accident that was a result of trial and error, he says.

Design

Hollis Brand Communication

Designers

Don Hollis, Gussue Bendeler

Client

Queensway Bay

A marketing and leasing program promotion for a coastal mixed-use retail project had to communicate a sense of a festive waterfront. Hollis Brand Communications' design incorporated embroidered sailcloth on the cover and rope holders from sail rigging as the binding. Both materials were found at a marine equipment store.

Design
Orlando Facioli Design

Metal cover
Sediro Inoue

Inside production
Printing Press

Client
Lycra Dupont

A plastic spiral binding might not be the first option a designer would consider for a metal-covered book. But the plastic coil is surprisingly strong, and it lets the brushed metal on the outside cover and the mirror-finished metal on the inside cover shine in this swimwear catalog. Designer Orlando Facioli says his main concerns with the design were safety and registration. His dummy has straight corners, which he discovered could be sharp. Also, it was difficult to register the holes punched in the cover with the holes punched into the inside pages. Each punching process had to be done on a different machine.

Design
Pensaré Design Group

Art director
Mary Ellen Velhow

Designer
Amy E. Billingham

Photography, production
Patrick Long

Printer
S&S Graphics

Client
Pensaré Design Group

For a self-promotional calendar, Pensaré Design Group took advantage of an art collection belonging to the company's president and creative director. So numerous were the art samples that the design team and printer were able to devise a split-page design that was also functional: Two weeks can be exposed at one time. The printer suggested Wire-o binding: It allows the split and full pages to be flipped back and forth easily, and it is a solid, stable centerpiece for the design.

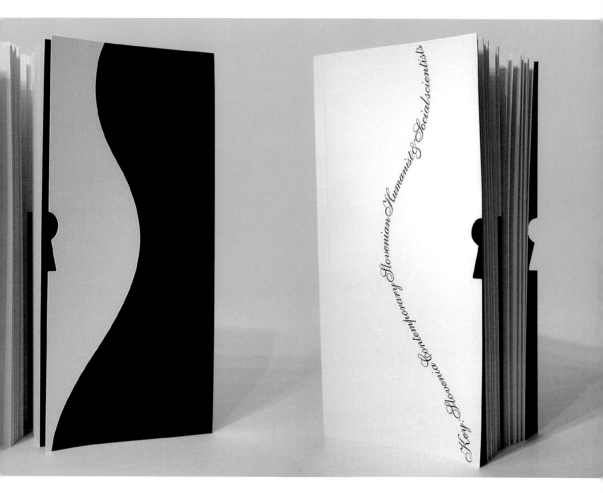

Design

Tomato Kosir

Client

Contemporary Slovenian
Humanists and Social
Scientists

This oversized booklet, created
by Tomato Kosir for the
Contemporary Slovenian
Humanists and Social Scientists,
was a giveaway publication
meant to address the two
groups within the membership.
It is bound on both sides, and it
is hinged at its center so it can
be folded back to form another
spine. Creating two outside
spines involves the same
process as creating just one,
but the pages on the right
side are trimmed down their
outside edge.

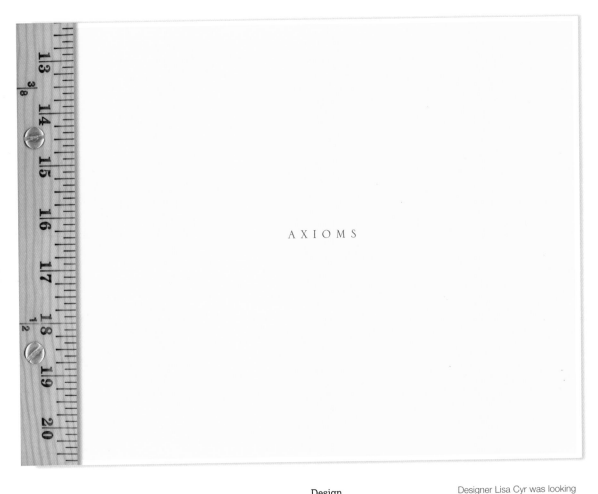

AXIOMS

Design
Red Canoe

Art director
Deb Koch

Designer
Caroline Kavanagh

Illustrator
Brian Cronin

Photography
DoubleTakes

Line art photographic overlays
Caroline Kavanagh, adapted from J. G. Heck

Copywriter
Lisa L. Cry

Title, heading, definition copy
Deb Koch

Client
Cyr Studio

Designer Lisa Cyr was looking for a way to attract the attention of clients in the graphic arts industries. With the help of the design office Red Canoe, she was able to build into the copy "rules" to which she frequently alludes in her writing and speaking: "Challenge," "Pursuit," and "Commitment." It made sense to incorporate an actual ruler into the binding of the book, which is drilled and bound with rivets.

Design
Hutchinson Associates, Inc.

Designer
Jerry Hutchinson

Printer, client
Dupli-Graphic Illinois

As substantial as this metal strip binding looks, it actually holds just two pages together: the two ends of an accordion-folded promotional book, and those ends are pasted on top of the aluminum strip. Nothing is contained or pinched together by the strip. The design was a continuation of a branding effort for Hutchinson Associates' client. Hutchinson had already produced a folder for the client with the same binding.

like silver snowflakes
melt upon yule log warm'd cheeks
cookies go so fast

PAUL KAJIWADA

potato latkes
don't last longer than xmas
i'll celebrate both

MICHELLE REGENBOGEN

Design, client
Michael Osborne Design

Michael Osborne Design used
a traditional binding method,
Japanese stab binding and a
bamboo skewer, to pull together
a holiday self-promotional gift
book of haiku. The 200-piece
run was letterpressed in
Osborne's own shop and
hand-assembled there as well.

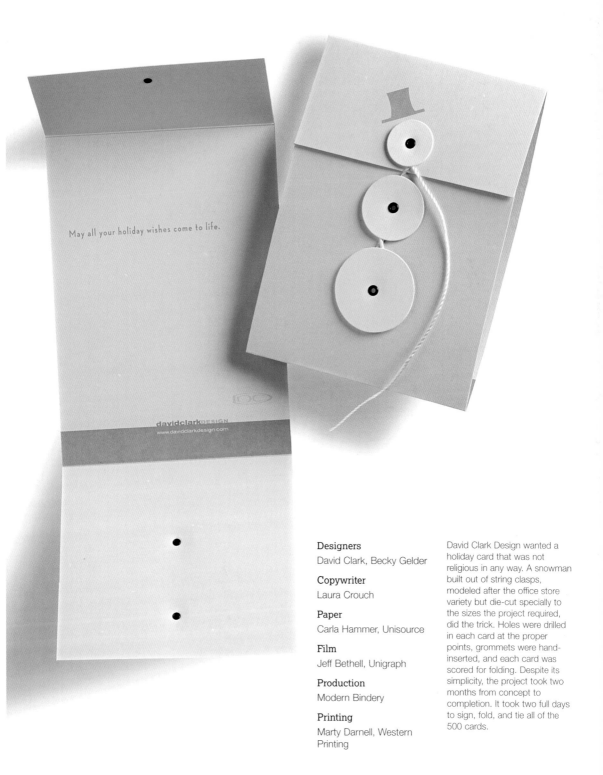

May all your holiday wishes come to life.

davidclarkDESIGN
www.davidclarkdesign.com

Designers
David Clark, Becky Gelder

Copywriter
Laura Crouch

Paper
Carla Hammer, Unisource

Film
Jeff Bethell, Unigraph

Production
Modern Bindery

Printing
Marty Darnell, Western
Printing

David Clark Design wanted a holiday card that was not religious in any way. A snowman built out of string clasps, modeled after the office store variety but die-cut specially to the sizes the project required, did the trick. Holes were drilled in each card at the proper points, grommets were hand-inserted, and each card was scored for folding. Despite its simplicity, the project took two months from concept to completion. It took two full days to sign, fold, and tie all of the 500 cards.

Designer
Shepardson Stern + Kaminsky

Printer, binder
Peter Kruty Editions

Client
Creative Artists Agency

This holiday greeting from Peter
Kruty Editions has an unusual
binding: The accordion-folded
piece is held together by a string
that runs through its center. The
card is built around the concept
of a spiritual thread that ties all
humankind together.

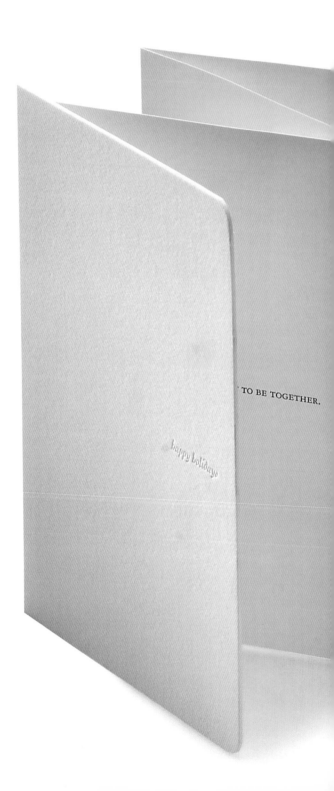

Chapter 4

Embossing, Debossing, Letterpress, and Engraving: Tactile Graphics

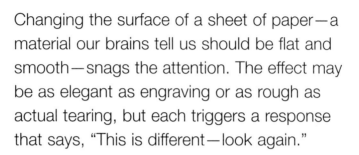

Changing the surface of a sheet of paper—a material our brains tell us should be flat and smooth—snags the attention. The effect may be as elegant as engraving or as rough as actual tearing, but each triggers a response that says, "This is different—look again."

Not only do people look twice, they are likely to feel the design several times as well. All of the surface effects described in this chapter create tactile graphics—and not only on paper. Today, with proper advice from an experienced pressperson, almost any malleable surface—cloth, metal, plastic—can be embossed, debossed, letterpressed, or engraved.

Types of Dies Used for Embossing and Debossing

- A *single-level* die produces an impression with a single depth. It is usually used for line art, lines, and any other single-dimension image that calls for a simple, well-defined edge.

- A *multilevel* die produces a dimensional imprint with several levels of depth.

- A *round-edged* die produces a soft edge on the imprint.

- A *beveled-edge* die combines the round, soft imprint with a well-defined edge. Beveled edges can have varying degrees of slope for different effects.

- A *sculptured* die has a variety of depths. It creates the most dimensional and realistic effect in its impressions.

Types of Embossing

- **Blind embossing** does not use ink or foil to highlight an embossed area. The result is a graphic effect that depends only on the dimensional quality of the imprint. Blind effects are wonderful and tactile, but be mindful that they will not show up on photocopies or faxes. In addition, almost any impression can be flattened by an aggressive laser printer. So keep the end use in mind.

- A **registered emboss** uses ink, foil, punching, or another embossed image, in register, to complete a graphic effect.

- Embossed graphics can be **pastelled** (also called tint-leaf embossing). A subtle foil is applied to the emboss at the same time it is imprinted, giving it a soft, antiqued look.

- Designers can choose to **glaze** a finished embossed area. In this process, heat is combined with

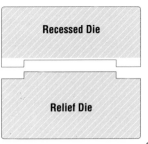

Single-level die

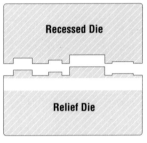

Multilevel die

Round-edged die

Beveled-edge die

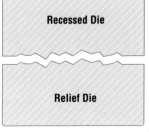

Sculptured die

pressure in the embossed area. The result is a shiny, burned impression.

- **Scorching** is another option. In this process, the temperature of the die heating plate is increased and a scorch produced in conjunction with the emboss. This is an effect that must be used with care and with the proper stock, as actual burning can occur. Also, text may become illegible.

Selecting the Right Materials to Emboss or Deboss

It is crucial for the designer to select the proper material for embossing or debossing; otherwise, the substrate may tear or break, the impression will be inadequate, or the substrate will be misshapen or warped. Long-fibered papers are best, particularly for deeper dies. In general, papers that work best with embossing and debossing are uncoated, heavy, and have a felt finish. The least subtle stocks are lightweight, recycled, or coated or varnished.

Embossing Type and Graphics

Special consideration must be given to type and graphics when they are embossed or debossed. Typically, embossing stretches type and images up and out, making them look larger than they actually are. Debossing has less effect, but it does tend to tighten kerning and other spacing a bit.

Try to set type in 12 points or above, and use lines thicker than 2 points. These effects tend to fill in tight or enclose areas; even serifs will not imprint well if they are not well defined. Screened items will not reproduce well using embossing or debossing; all art should be produced as line art. Finally, embosses and debosses that are too close to the edges of a sheet will cause warping: Stay at least 1/2 inch (1.3 cm) away from any edge.

Engraving

Engraving is an ancient craft that speaks of elegance and sophistication. It feels substantial. In fact, the easiest way to know if a design has been engraved is to look at the area around the impression area. A flattened halo around the printed area is a tell-tale sign of engraving. The viewer can see and feel the process.

With engraving, text or art is etched into a copper, steel, or magnesium plate. A mirror-image counter is also produced. The plate is coated with ink, filling the etched areas, and the printing surface is pressed between the plate and the counter, creating an image with a slightly raised impression. The indentation one feels on the back of a sheet is caused by the pressure exerted by the printing press when it forces the paper into engraved areas on a plate. Engraving inks are opaque and can be color matched to almost any shade. They are available in fluorescent and metallic shades as well.

Today, it's possible to engrave on surfaces other than paper. Laser engraving can be used to cut into nearly any surface; a computer controls the laser's movement.

Paper Selection

The traditional engraving process exerts about 2 tons (1.8 metric tons) of pressure per square inch, so selecting the proper paper is essential; papers with high cotton content are common choices. Any long-fibered paper that can handle the stretch will work. Uncoated papers are best: Coated papers will crack.

Engraving speaks of elegance and longevity. It's an excellent design tool in these days of virtual business: Whereas websites are ethereal, engraving is concrete and lasting: You can actually feel it with your fingers. It's also environmentally smart, as the inks used by the process are water based.

tip

Engraving is a good option for any document that must be secure, as it is not easily counterfeited.

Good Advice for Good Results

- *Tiny details, fine lines, and small type are preserved by the process. One exception may be engraving with metallic inks: The powders used in metallic inks may not be ground fine enough.*

- *Lines ½ point or less can cause paper to buckle when engraved. Any lines that intersect may cause a buildup at the junction.*

- *Halftones do not work well in engraving.*

- *Engraving inks are opaque, so they are ideal for printing on dark or textured stock. Colors remain true.*

- *Multiple-color jobs require separate print passes for each color.*

- *Engraving is a slow, costly process, so plan ahead in budgeting and scheduling.*

- *The maximum plate area for engraving is 5 × 9 inches (12.7 × 22.9 cm), but the maximum image size is 4 × 8 inches (10.2 × 20.3 cm).*

- *To print large flat or screened areas, consult carefully with the printer first.*

- *It is possible to engrave on both sides of a sheet, but be mindful that both impressions will affect both sides of the sheet.*

- *Engraving should be the last step in any multifunction print run to avoid inadvertently flattening it. The only exception is when a design also includes embossing or debossing (especially blind embossing or debossing). In that case, those processes should be last. Also, it is sometimes better to engrave envelopes before they are assembled.*

- *Laser printing on an engraved design may flatten or otherwise diminish the engraved effect.*

Letterpress

Letterpress is the relief print process Johannes Gutenberg was using in 1450. Ink rollers touch the top of raised images—type or plates—to ink them in preparation for direct impression onto a printing surface. The result, as the graphics are pressed into a sheet, is a depressed or debossed, tactile feel.

The majority of presses are 10 × 15 inches (25.4 × 38.1 cm) or 13 × 18 inches (33 × 45.7 cm); the largest available is 29 × 41 inches (73.7 × 104.1 cm). Presses can be open and flat, or they can open and close like a clamshell. Any size of paper (or other substrate) may be used as long as it fits the press—anything from glassine to heavy chipboard. Substrates that are absolutely nonporous are not a good choice for letterpress.

Preparing art and type for letterpress printing can be done in several ways. Traditionally, letterpress is achieved with handset type, rules, and art elements from which a camera-ready proof is made for plating. Alternatively, just about any computer file can be converted into a magnesium, photopolymer (plastic), or copper plate that, in turn, can be used for printing. The digital approach is probably easier and more expedient—more fonts are likely available, halftones are a snap to create, and other art elements are more plentiful—although the traditional way, arguably, yields more interesting results. Plates are best for longer runs or longer documents, however.

Designer Bennett Holzworth of Be a Design Group says he has had fun printing on just about every kind of paper. "If you want the fine irregularities of the wood type to show up, print on a smooth paper. If you want a deep impression, chose a thick, textured paper—120 pounds is nice," he says. Art and printmaking papers take ink and impression better than commercially made papers, but these are more expensive. Be careful when printing on any new or different material, Holzworth says. "A deep impression could easily smash delicate and hard-to-find metal type. You are better off experimenting with plates."

Registration with letterpress can be dead-on with newer, motorized presses. With a person-powered or antique press, it's a good idea to allow for more spoilage when registration is not spot-on.

Holzworth uses polymer plates that allows for very fine detail—down to .1-point line and down to 2-point Times New Roman. Michael Goodman, of Dickson's, Inc., a printing firm well-versed in letterpress printing, advises keeping type no smaller than 6 point and lines no smaller than .5 point. "Always contact your printer prior to starting your design process," adds Goodman.

Bruce Licher of Independent Project Press can successfully print up to a 110-line screen without screen clogging on press. Halftone screens will letterpress better on a coated or smooth stock, he notes. "If you want to print a halftone or heavy solid on something like chipboard, put down a coat of another ink first," Licher adds.

Any color of ink that is available for offset printing is available for letterpress printing. Some letterpress inks are oil- or soy oil–based, but some are rubber-based. The latter take longer to dry—but, says Licher, "opaque white in a rubber-based ink is much brighter than white oil-based ink, so it's better for printing on chipboard or dark stock. But you'll have to let it dry for a week." Rubber-based ink yields a matte finish, whereas oil-based inks are glossy. Multiple coats of oil-based produce an almost varnished effect.

Letterpress printing takes longer than standard offset printing, particularly if the printer is using a hand-fed press. Also, with a hand-fed press, there is likely to be more variation in inking and registration within the same run. But for many designers, the hand-made effect is well worth the wait.

Design
And Partners

Creative director
David Schimmel

Designer
Ashleigh Lindenauer

Client
Ransom Everglades School

At the Ransom Everglades School, there is a tradition for members of the student body to leave behind personal imprints. For a capital campaign folder aimed at alumni and parents, the designers at And Partners decided to borrow from that tradition and create a uniquely debossed cover: an impression taken from a black-and-white photo of a new cement block with actual inscriptions. The die for the strike was hand-sculpted from brass.

Design
Blu Concept, Inc.

Creative director
Rik Klingle-Watt

Designer
Jennifer Taylor Paravantes

Printer
Printing Ink

Embosser
Trade Engraving

Shaktea is a funky tea lounge in an up-and-coming fashion district in Vancouver, British Columbia. Its beautiful, sculpted embossed business card, part of a larger identity system, feels romantic and exotic, speaking clearly of the faraway places from which tea comes. Rik Klinger-Watt says the embossing required extra-special attention. "Make sure artwork, type, and rules are not only thick enough but spaced wide enough apart to permit a good impression. We deliberately went with lines that were thin, almost wispy, but we made subtle adjustments to the emboss art so it would work. We also sent actual-size hard copies to the embosser before creating the final art so they could review and troubleshoot what might have been problem areas," he says.

Design
Blok Design

Designers
Vanessa Eckstein, Vanessa Enriquez

Client
Marco

This invitation for an art exhibition titled "Only the Characters Change," at the Marco Museum, was embossed into a color-shifting, highly reflective thermoplastic film. "Each invite becomes a reflection of the person receiving it, in constant motion, shifting in color depending on the light and heat that surrounds him," says designer Vanessa Eckstein. "We wanted the tactile aspect of embossing. Also, the text appears and disappears from the invitation."

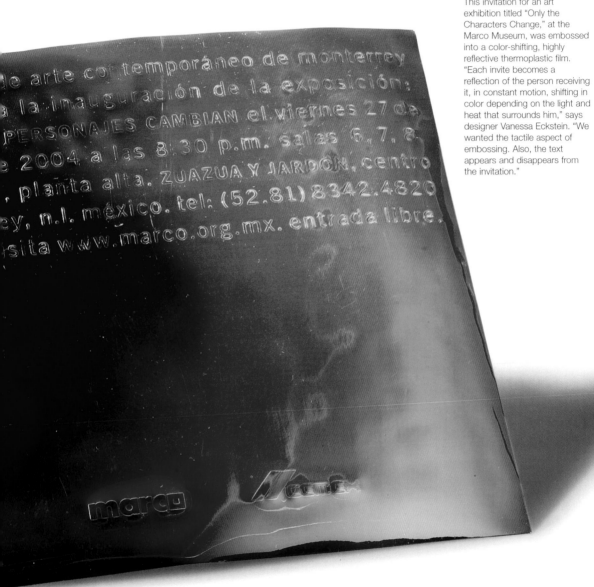

Design
Michael Osborne Design

Client
Jack Daniel's

Embossing need not be reserved for paper or plastic. Here, Michael Osborne Design embossed a metal label. The most challenging aspect of this design was getting the typography just right, says Osborne. "The kerning and word spacing had to be set to allow for the fact that the type would stretch when embossed," he says.

feed me

Design
Bruketa&Zinic

Art directors, designers
Davor Bruketa, Nikola Zinic

Photographers
Marin Topic, Domagoi Kunic

Production
IBL d.o.o.

Production heads
Boris Matesic, Luka Saric

Client
Podravka

Bruketa&Zinic used embossed plastic for the cover of a highly unusual annual report, titled "Feed Me," for Podravka, a large food company. The hole in the heart, combined with the title, encourages the viewer to put his or her whole heart into everything. (Inside pages of this report are shown on pages 114–115.)

Design
Blu Concept, Inc.

Creative director
Rik Klingle-Watt

Designer
Lindsay Rankin

Copywriter
John Vigna

Printer
Glenmore Printing

Blu Concept was originally contacted by the BC Cancer Foundation to create a simple program for an evening benefit, but after hearing the story of the late young woman to whom the evening was dedicated, the design firm's pro bono efforts ramped up to this beautiful, embossed purple velvet book that contains a music CD and booklet. The logo on the cover was embossed on the velvet after the fabric was mounted on the book board,

Design
Spiral Design

Concept
Tobi Saulnier, 1st Playable

Creative director
Neil Wright

Designers
Emily Rawitsch, Neil Wright, Anne Hobday

Illustration
Anne Hobday

Printing, band
Crazy Aaron's Putty World

Printing, labels
Greenbush Label and Tape

Putty, tin
Crazy Aaron's Putty World

Client
Spiral Design

Embossing doesn't have to be hard. For this imaginative, interactive promotion, thermochromatic clay was hand-stamped by Spiral Design Studio with the client's message. The design reflects 1st Playable's corporate culture and youth-focused market.

Design

Karen Bartolomei, Grapevine

Printer

Peter Kruty Editions

Client

Leila Bay Sayegh, Andres Alvarez

This elaborate save-the-date announcement for a wedding celebration was challenging because of its scale. Printed on a large poster letterpress that can print up to 31 × 56 inch (78.7 × 142.2 cm) sheets, the design uses an all-cotton heavyweight printmaking paper that took the letterpress impression beautifully. But the natural stretch of the paper caused problems for the two-color registration, which the printer solved by keeping the packing on the press exactly the same for all runs. Even the scoring had to be extremely precise, as each fold in the accordion-style piece depended on the proceeding one.

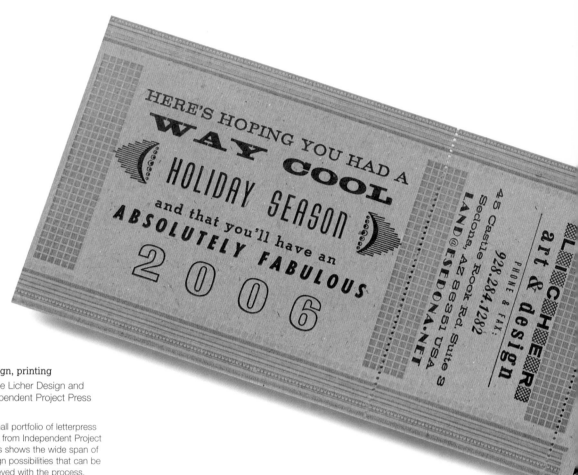

Design, printing

Bruce Licher Design and
Independent Project Press

A small portfolio of letterpress
work from Independent Project
Press shows the wide span of
design possibilities that can be
achieved with the process.
Designer and printer Bruce
Licher printed these samples on
two Chandler & Price platen
presses and a Vandercook
proofing press.

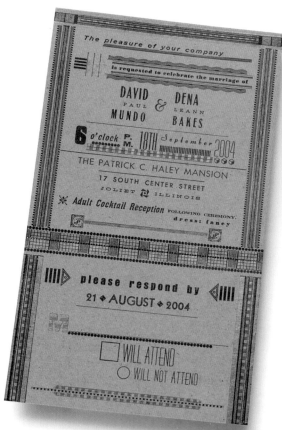

More letters samples from Independent Project Press

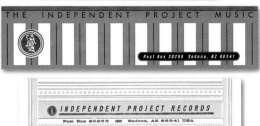

Chapter 5

Cut Work: Die-Cuts, Perforations, and Kiss-Cuts

Maybe it's that magic a child feels from unfolding an intricate snowflake cut from a flat sheet of paper. Maybe it's because scissors are such a universal, easy-to-master tool.

The ability to manipulate paper—and for professional designers, just about any other substrate—in such a fundamental way is indeed magic. One piece of paper becomes two, or shapes emerge from its surface, or it becomes able to link to something else.

Cutting is such a simple action, but it yields profound results, whether they are aesthetic or practical.

Die-Cutting

Die-cutting is using a die to completely or partially cut out shapes or areas of a substrate, usually after printing but before the assembly of a design. Defined as a finishing process by printers, die-cutting is also called dinking or blanking in trades other than graphic design, such as the automotive, medical, packaging, or industrial fields.

Die-cutting can be as simple as cutting two slits in a piece of paper to hold a business card in place or as complicated as a pop-up book. It can also be used with cloth or three-dimensional constructions.

Almost any shape can be die-cut into paper or other soft and hard surfaces. A quick Web search of "die-cutting" reveals plenty of nonpaper options—metal, rubber, cloth, and much more—that might be incorporated into a graphic design.

Die-Cutting Methods

Most die-cuts are made using one of three methods:

1. Sharp steel rules are formed or bent to match a shape on a film positive. These rules are then pressed through paper into a wood base. This method is limited, though, as the rules may not bend into exact corners or perfect circles. Designers are also limited by the radius of the bend—the minimum is normally $3/16$ inch (4.8 mm)—as well as the inability to strip out waste from the die-cut by removing the unwanted portions of the paper.

2. The second method delivers more intricate and exact shapes by using cutting edges produced by acid-etching metal plates. These carry a photographic image taken from the art, so they are exact reproductions of the original design.

3. The third and most precise option is laser die-cutting, which can cut paper as well as plastics, leather, metals, fiberglass, and just about anything else imaginable. Laser die-cutting is usually reserved for elaborate or intricate cuts, but because it is extremely accurate, it is a useful process for any design that has close tolerances or tight registration requirements. The price of laser cutting has decreased as the technology has improved, so it can be a very attractive option. There are cautions, however: The laser in this technique burns the unwanted paper away, so the remaining paper may be discolored or scorched. The finer the image to be cut, the less pronounced the scorching will be.

Raster Lasers versus Vector Lasers

There are two basic laser-cutting systems in general use: raster lasers (scanning) and vector (X-Y) lasers. The most complex cuts can be done with a scanning laser that vaporizes the entire area of stock to be removed. This system, which is best suited to cutting paper and not other materials, uses paper handling similar to a conventional sheet-fed press and is compatible with most other offline processes. Detail is limited to areas of art that are as large as the thickness of the stock being cut. It is even possible to cut a screened photographic image as a series of extremely small holes. The amount of detail does not affect the cost. However, because scanning lasers burn away unwanted paper, scorching can occur. The smoky effect can be controlled, to some extent, by paper choice.

A perforating cylinder place cuts—small or large—right in the paper as it moves through the press.

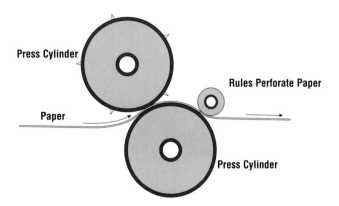

Press Cylinder

Rules Perforate Paper

Paper

Press Cylinder

Design Notes

> *Tom Hutchings, designer for Form: Design and Art Direction of London, needed the accuracy of a scanning laser for his company's New Year's greeting card, but had to work around burns that might result on the stock he selected: a mirror board with a shiny, reflective surface on one side and flat white paper on the other. He set the laser to cut through the design through from the shiny side so the card front would remain clean.*

Vector laser systems, on the other hand, cut around the areas that are later removed as scrap. This system is ideal for cutting wood, acrylic, Mylar, and other thick or inorganic materials. The stock is held in place on a vacuum table in a lift of up to six sheets, depending on stock weight. One set of mechanisms moves the stock, and another moves the laser, which is always kept perpendicular to the sheets.

Design Notes

> *Hutchings offers this caution about X-Y laser cutting: "You should be aware that the process can cause a long turnaround, as the work has to be laser cut after printing and before it is trimmed or creased." Scanning lasers, however, are often the last process in any series of offline operations.*

Perforations

"Perfing" is similar to die-cutting, but it cuts through paper fibers in designated segments. A perf at the top of a check, for example, allows it to be removed easily from a checkbook. Perfs can be composed of straight, dashed lines (as on a check), or can be made from a series of shapes like circles or ovals (as on a postage stamp).

Perforating rules are placed right on a press cylinder; as paper travels through the press, it is struck by the rules. Printers describe perforations by bursting strength or ties per inch (TPI). The tie (or tab) is the part of the perforation where the paper is not cut: It still ties the paper together. Tie areas are usually shorter than cut areas so the paper will tear easily at the perf, but this depends on the end use of the design and the paper specified. A TPI of 4 or 6 means the paper will tear very easily. A TPI of 16 or 18 is much stronger; in fact, it must be folded and sometimes waggled back and forth to induce the tear, like an insert card in a magazine.

It's also possible to specify a letter-edge perforation. This perf is almost invisible. When the paper is separated, a clean, smooth edge remains. Letter-edge perfs have a TPI from 50 to 72.

Kiss-Cutting

Kiss-cutting is very like die-cutting, but the steel cutting rule cuts through the front of the piece and only "kisses" the back. Sheets of stickers are generally kiss-cut, as are adhesive postage stamps; the die cuts through the adhesive stock but not the backing. Kiss-cutting can also be used to introduce a line for a fold. Instead of bruising or denting paper fibers the way a rule strike or scoring die does, a kiss-cut actually introduces a shallow cut to the fibers, weakening the paper in that area and increasing the chance it will fold in that spot.

Custom versus Preexisting Dies

Printers and production houses that provide die-cutting, kiss-cutting, and perforating generally have a library of stock dies in standard shapes: slits for business cards, circles, folder blanks, rectangular window shapes for envelopes, line patterns, and more whimsical shapes such as hearts and suns. Ask to see the complete library; there may be a shape from a previous job that will work for you, too. Some suppliers post their collection in a downloadable form, so you can lay it right over your design as you work.

Design Notes

> *It's possible to custom design a die, but this option is expensive and time-consuming. When IE Design + Communications, of Hermosa Beach, California, created a simple and elegant identity for Theresa Kathryn, a company that manufactures a distinctly feminine, business-oriented line of products, its designers discovered that a custom die added about three to four weeks to production of the client's die-cut and foil-stamped stationery system.*

"A die-cut 1/2 inch (1.3 cm) or smaller requires an electronic digital mastering machine, which can be hard to find. The lead time is long for the mold," says IE's Kenny Goldstein.

With a really complex project, it may pay to investigate many die-cutting providers.

Gee + Chung, of San Francisco, created a unique identity for Give Something Back International, a not-for-profit organization, and costs were a concern. With die-cuts and spot colors involved, Earl Gee and Fani Chung could not find a U.S. supplier that could provide the intricately cut folders and business cards they needed at a cost they could afford. So they took the job overseas, which added to the schedule but saved plenty of money.

Of course, working long-distance creates other concerns. "When working with overseas printers, prepare a test file to check your screen values, colors, and images, and request your printer to run a press proof. This will provide an accurate proof to match in the event that you cannot actually check the job in person," advises Gee.

Schedule Considerations

The prep time for a die-cutting process is long. Any designer would be wise to build in time for discussion and experimentation with the die-cutting provider, including building an exact dummy of the finished piece. The time to find problems is weeks before the job is put on press, not after valuable stock has been irrevocably cut or trimmed. As the saying goes, "Measure twice, cut once."

When paper stock is ordered, it must come to an acceptable moisture level for the cutting process, as with any finishing or print process. This waiting period can be particularly lengthy if a design is printed at one facility and then shipped to a second facility for cutting; the design must assume the proper relative humidity twice. Stock that is too dry will crack, and some coated stocks or laid stock will not cut well.

tip

Don't forget that whatever you die-cut into the front of a sheet will also appear on the back of the sheet. If anything appears underneath or behind the die-cut area, it should make sense with the cut.

How to Spec a Die

The most important thing to do when specifying a die cut, perforation, or kiss-cut is to ask the printer or production house you have chosen for its instructions. Every establishment is different and has different requirements for its machines.

Usually, though, it is best to provide a design file in line only—that is, with no fills, no written instructions, and no other markings that are unnecessary for the production of the cuts. Remember: At this stage, they are producing a die with which to make the cuts, not printing the design. Build the cutting or scoring file on a separate layer, so any changes can be easily adjusted and the file can be sent to the die-maker without images.

Clearly differentiate all cut lines from other lines in the design. Adobe Illustrator's Overprint Stroke option (in the Attributes palette) allows you to assign a color to cut lines that is different from any other lines designated; a fold line, for instance, should have its own color. Alternatively, use a dashed line to indicate scoring or folding and a solid line for cutting. A 1-point line is generally sufficient. An Adobe Illustrator file or other EPS file will work with your die cutter's program (this is usually a CAD setup). Layout files (such as those from Quark XPress) don't work, as they are not easily manipulated. Ask the die-cutter if you need to flop the design (make it backward), or if the production staff will do that in house.

Remove any hidden layers or embedded elements before you share files with the printer. Even if they are not visible on screen, the die maker's computer will see them, and delays on press may occur. Additionally, don't include written instructions in the die-cut file; send these on a separate file or with your printout of the files.

Often, designers will specify a registered die-cut. This means the cut must line up exactly with something underneath or behind it. This is another instance where working closely with your printer will pay in the end.

Paper Selection

The eventual success or failure of a die-cut, kiss-cut, or perforated design is heavily dependent on the paper you select. In general, uncoated papers perform best for any kind of cutting.

Paper grain is a major consideration. Even a hefty perforation running across the grain of a heavy sheet of paper will yield a ragged tear. A sample of the stock should be shown to the printer or die maker to determine which type of perforation rule should be used. Talk to your die cutter for the best advice for specific projects.

If a paper has a special coating or backing, or if it already has something like foil stamping or thermography applied, die-cutting may not be a good choice. These treatments will crack or split when cut or scored, so it is best to make cuts in an unembellished area of the design.

Design Notes

> *Before going to press with an elaborate pop-up book with many die-cuts, Voice Design creates dummies to try out different paper stocks. "Working samples with various weights of stock will provide the best results for making decisions," says Scott Carslake, art director at the Adelaide, Australia, design firm. "Do not simply guess." In addition, to produce something as specialized as a pop-up book, it's good to work with a manufacturer that specializes in pop-ups.*

Designer Stefan Sagmeister created an elaborate die-cut design as a wedding invitation for friends. The design is not printed at all; its concept is carried solely by a thin series of cuts and die-cut words. To make sure the design could indeed be cut, Sagmeister sent test files with many shapes of tiny type, cuts, and scores. The laser cutter tried each test and then let him know where type had to be sized up to achieve the desired results.

Good Advice for Great Results

- A design on paper with lots of dark coating or ink on it, when kiss-cut or die-cut, will reveal its still light or white middle. This can be an interesting design effect, but if a creamy center is not part of the concept, it is best to stick with a colored stock.

- If a printed sheet has dark coverage on one side and light coverage on the other, die-cut into the heavy side to minimize chipping on the ink.

- It's important to think about function. Some die-cuts, especially those with angles, may be destined to catch on everything they brush against. Imagine a die-cut star on a book jacket: Every time it is slid in and out of a stack of books, it is bound to snag on something and rip, spoiling the original design.

- Die-cuts on mailings must proceed unscathed through the postal service as well, so use caution in these instances.

- Die-cut pieces sometimes have nicks on them. These are small nibs on the die-cut edges that are left by nicks in the knife edge. The nibs must be in place or else the sheet, when cut, would fall apart on press; the nibs hold the waste in place until it is stripped from the finished sheet. The trouble is, the nicks do show in the final design. A talented printer or production artist may know how to hide them as part of the final design, so ask for advice.

- Avoid die-cutting too close to the edge of a sheet of the paper to avoid puckers or tears.

- Keep text or other information at least $1/4$ inch (6 mm) away from any cut.

- Especially complicated die-cutting is sometimes done overseas. Keep the extra time for shipping and proofing in the schedule. Also remember that shipments will incur extra freight, postages, and duties when they enter the country.

- Remember that steel rules cannot be bent at 90-degree angles. They must be mitered together, and this can cause a nick.

Designers
Ruth Huimerind, Jyri Lovn

Paper skirt
Krista Leesi

Copywriter
Peeter Sauter

Printer
K-Print

Client
MODO Paper

This paper skirt was hand-cut out of plain copy paper as part of a photo-illustration created for a Modo Paper (now called MAP) Christmas brochure. "It's possible to do nice things from simple paper," says Ruth Huimerind, designer for the piece.

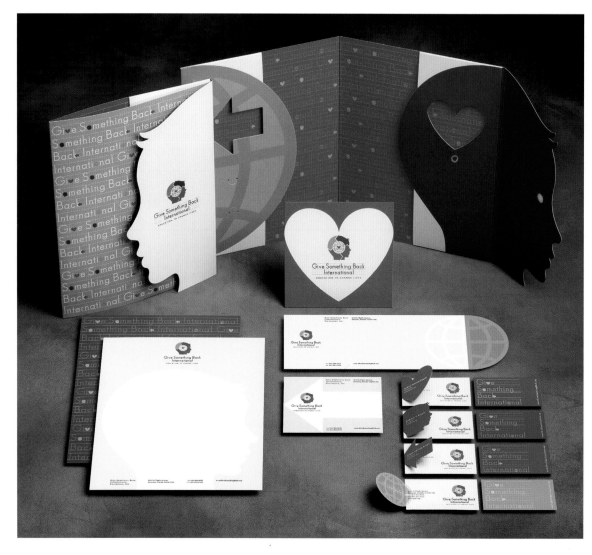

Design

Gee + Chung Design

Art director, designer, illustrator

Earl Gee

Printer

Quality Printing, Ltd. (Hong Kong)

Gee + Chung created a colorful identity full of symbols for Give Something Back International, a not-for-profit that provides life-changing educational opportunities for children in need worldwide. It is a system with many die-cuts and multiple PMS colors. Earl Gee suggests cutting from the heavy coverage side to minimize chipping in the heavier ink. Also, he and partner Fani Chung provided their printer with a test file that could be run to check out all colors, screen values, and images before the complicated job went on press.

Design
Hutchinson Associates, Inc.

Designer
Jerry Hutchinson

Printer
Darwill Press and Dupli-Graphic

This informational folder's design was inspired by the company's logo; it actually replicates it. Each divider page inside has a rounded top, cut in the same way a folder is stamped out, says Jerry Hutchinson of Hutchinson Associates. It was not a complicated job, but special care was taken with the photo to make sure the cut pieces could be inserted easily not only at the printer's facility but at the recipient's office as well. Specifying a thicker paper (Starwhite Vicksburg was used here) results in smoother, more stable die-cut job, and it produces a solid feeling that reflects well on the client.

Design
IE Design + Communications

Creative director
Marcie Carson

Logo designers
Kenny Goldstein, Jane Lee

Stationery designer
Jane Lee

Printer
Roadrunner Press

IE Design + Communications created an identity for Theresa Kathryn, a company that produces a feminine line of business goods, that is bold, sophisticated, modern, classic, and feminine. Rather than print the logo of the business card and letterhead, the designers decided to die-cut it. The cut's small size and intricate shape required them to locate a die cutter with an electronic digital mastering machine, and the mastering added three to four weeks to the job's schedule. A heavy paper (Starwhite 110 pound for the card and 80 pound for the letterhead) maintains the crisp cut and keeps the individual pieces stable.

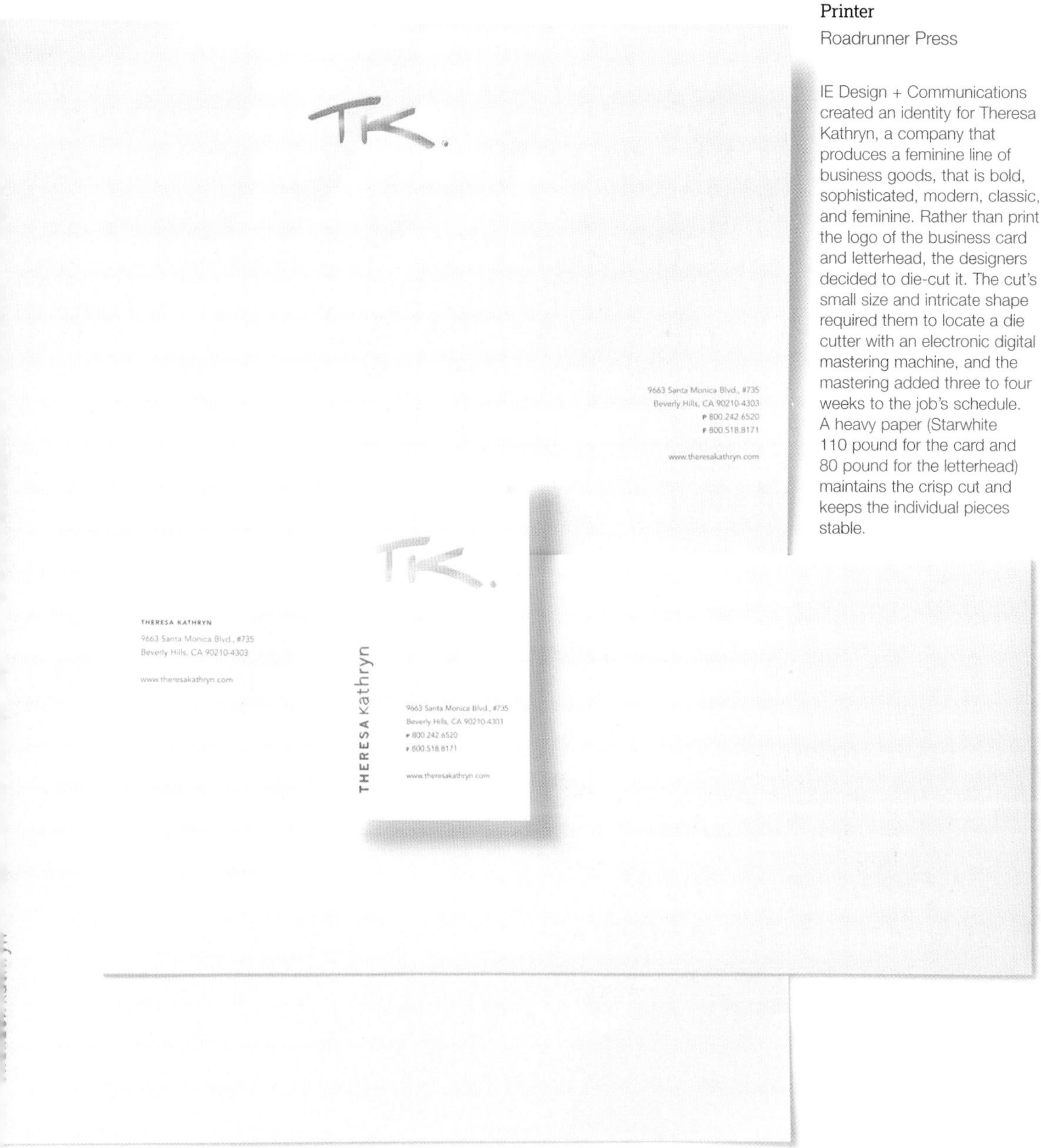

TK.

9663 Santa Monica Blvd., #735
Beverly Hills, CA 90210-4303
P 800.242.6520
F 800.518.8171

www.theresakathryn.com

THERESA KATHRYN
9663 Santa Monica Blvd., #735
Beverly Hills, CA 90210-4303

www.theresakathryn.com

THERESA kathryn

9663 Santa Monica Blvd., #735
Beverly Hills, CA 90210-4303
P 800.242.6520
F 800.518.8171

www.theresakathryn.com

Design
Bruketa&Zinic

Art directors, designers
Davor Bruketa, Nikola Zinic

Photographers
Marin Topic, Domagoj Kunic

Production
IBL d.o.o.

Production heads
Boris Matesic, Luka Saric

These pages are from an annual report for Podravka, a large regional food company in Croatia. Bruketa&Zinic has a tradition of creating innovative reports for this client. For this design, the company's logo—a heart—played a major part. Young people, with literal holes in their hearts, were shown to say, "Feed me." The report is full of recipes that answer the plea. These die-cuts are made more dimensional as they are backed by blank paper and create a noticeable gap that furthers the "hole in the heart" idea.

Design

Paul West, Andy Harvey

Client

Form: Design and
Art Direction

Form: Design and Art Direction
used laser cutting and mirror
board to produce this unusual
card. To avoid burn marks on
the white side of the paper, the
laser was directed through the
mirrored side. In addition, says
designer Tom Hutchings, to
make sure no part of the design
fell out during the laser-cutting
process, his team designed a
font that contained no counters
in the letters and that was thick
enough to be lasered. Laser
cutting can add a lot of time to
the process; this design had to
be cut before it was trimmed
and creased.

Design
Leng Soh, Pann Lim, Roy Poh, Carolyn Teo, Cat Phua

Die cutter, printer
Colourscan PTE Ltd.

Client
Tate

To mimic an architectural element in their client's new luxury apartments, Kinetic designers specified Star Dream 300 gsm paper, a tough but shimmering textured paper that looks like metal and could withstand this intricate laser die-cut. The die-cut casts shadows on the preceding and following page, similar to the way the actual metal architectural element in the building creates its own shadows. For repeated patterns, a laser cut is the best choice, reports designer Roy Poh.

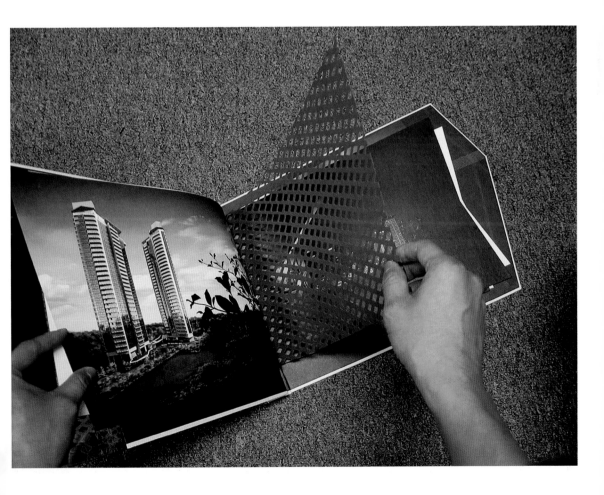

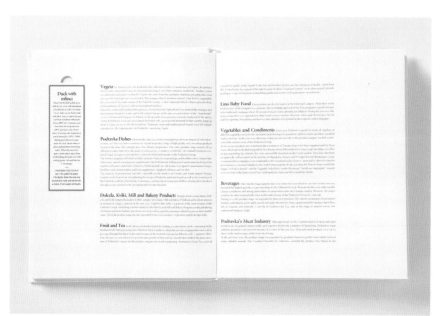

Design
Bruketa&Zinic

Art directors, designers
Davor Bruketa, Nikola Zinic

Photographers
Marin Topic, Domagoj Kunic

Production
IBL d.o.o.

Productions heads
Boris Matesic, Luka Saric

In other sections of Bruketa &Zinic's Podravka annual report, the designers used perforations to create a unique interactive element. A die-cut fingerhold encourages the reader to open a little door on a number of pages. Inside, the reader is rewarded with more information.

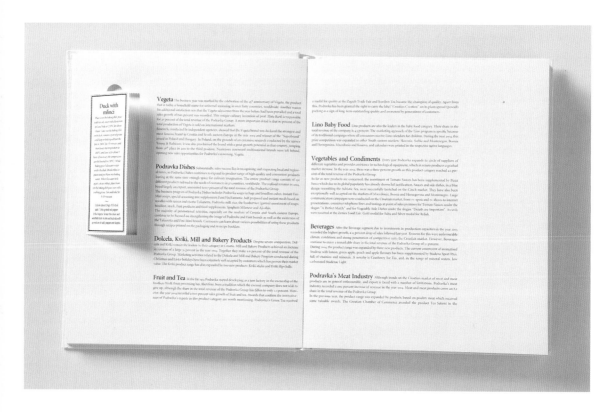

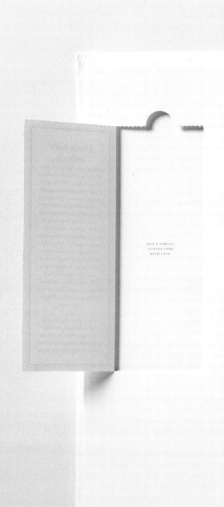

DON'T FORGET,
ALWAYS COOK
WITH LOVE.

Vegeta

The business year was marked by the celebration of the 45th anniversary of Vegeta, the product that is today a household name for universal seasoning in over forty countries, worldwide. Another reason for additional satisfaction was that the Vegeta sales crises from the year before had been prevailed and a total sales growth of two percent was recorded. This unique culinary invention of prof. Zlata Bartl is responsible for 20 percent of the total revenue of the Podravka Group. A more important detail is that 80 percent of the total production of Vegeta is sold on international markets.

Research, conducted by independent agencies, showed that the Vegeta brand was declared the strongest and most famous brand in Croatia and South-eastern Europe in the year 2004 and winner of the "Superbrand" award in Poland and Hungary. In Poland, on the grounds of an extensive research conducted by the agency Young & Rubicam, it was also proclaimed the brand with a great growth potential in that country, jumping from 28th place in 2001 to the third position. Numerous renowned multinational brands were left behind, opening new sales opportunities for Podravka's seasoning, Vegeta.

Podravka Dishes

Substantially, sales success lies in recognising and respecting local and regional tastes, so Podravka Dishes continues to expand its product range of high quality and convenient products leaving at the same time enough space for culinary imagination. The entire product range consists of 230 different products tailored to the needs of customers in 37 countries, worldwide. The realised revenue in 2004, based largely on export, amounted to 6.7 percent of the total revenue of the Podravka Group.

The business program of Podravka Dishes includes Podravka soups in bags and bouillon cubes, instant Fini-Mini soups, special seasoning mix supplements Fant/Fix/Fantastic, half prepared and instant meals based on noodles with sauces and risotto Talianetta, Podravka milk rice, the foodservice (gastro) assortment of soups, bouillon, stock, Fant products and food supplements, Spaghetti Milanese and Aji-shio.

The majority of promotional activities, especially on the markets of Croatia and South-eastern Europe, continue to be focused on strengthening the image of Podravka and Fant brands as well as the awareness of the Talianetta and Fini-Mini brands. Customers can learn about various possibilities of using these products through recipes printed on the packaging and in recipe booklets.

Dolcela, Kviki, Mill and Bakery Products

Despite severe competition, Dolcela and Kviki remain the leaders in their category in Croatia. Mill and Bakery Products achieved an increase in revenue of a large 35 percent in the year 2004. Together they make 6.6 percent of the total revenue of the Podravka Group. Marketing activities related to the Dolcela and Mill and Bakery Program conducted during Christmas and Easter holidays have been extremely well accepted by customers which has proven their market value. The Kviki product range has also expanded by two new products: Kviki sticks and Kviki flips balls.

Fruit and Tea

In the far 1934 Podravka started developing as a jam factory in the ownership of the brothers Wolf. Fruit processing has, therefore, been a tradition which the current company does not wish to give up, although the share in the total revenue of the Podravka Group has fallen to only 2.1 percent. However, the year 2004 recorded a two percent sales growth of fruit and tea. Awards that confirm the innovativeness of Podravka's experts in this product category are worth mentioning. Podravka's Green Tea received

a medal for quality at the Zagreb [...] this. Podravka has been granted th[...] packing as a sign of long-term out[...]

Lino Baby Food

Lino [...] total revenue of the company is 4.9[...] of its traditional campaign where a[...] prize competition was expanded t[...] and Herzegovina, Macedonia and [...]

Vegetables and Co[...]

different vegetables and provides a[...] market increase. In the year 2004, [...] cent of the total revenue of the Po[...] As far as new products are conce[...] Sauce which due to its global popu[...] design resembling the Adriatic Se[...] exceptionally well accepted on the [...] communication campaigns were c[...] presentations, consumer telephon[...] slogan "A Perfect Match" and for [...] were received at the Zenica Food [...]

Beverages

After the Bever[...] recorded the highest growth, a 15 p[...] climate conditions and strong pe[...] continue to enjoy a remarkable sh[...] During 2004, the product range wa[...] Studena with lemon, green apple, [...] full of vitamins and minerals. A [...] carbonated Studenac Light.

Podravka's Meat I[...]

products are in general unfavour [...] industry recorded a one percent i[...] share in the total revenue of the Po[...] In the previous year, the product [...] some valuable awards. The Croa[...]

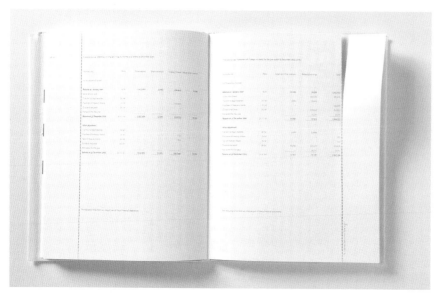

Design
Bruketa&Zinic

Art directors, designers
Davor Bruketa, Nikola Zinic

Photographers
Marin Topic, Domagoj Kunic

Production, printing
IBL d.o.o.

Production head
Boris Matesic

Bruketa&Zinic used perforation in a different way for another Podravka annual report. Doubled-over pages are bound in with their folds on the outside of the book, but some pages have a perf running down their edge. When the perf is separated, the reader finds more detailed information relating to the topic on the front of the sheet.

TWIST PATTY

40 dg turkey breasts, 25 dg turkey liver, 25 dg butter, 3 dg dry bacon, 1 Vegeta tablespoon for turkey, 1dl cream, grated nutmeg, 3-4 sour cucumber, 2 tablespoons cognac, 2 tablespoons lemon juice, Cut turkey meat and liver into cubes and fry on 5 dg butter. Add cut bacon and Vegeta Twist for turkey, stew adding water until tender. Cool meat and liver and then grind. Mix rest of butter, add ground meat and liver, cream, grated cucumbers, nutmegs, lemon juice to combine well. Put the patty mixture into a long mould or smaller ones, cool. Remove cooled patty from moulds and serve with toast.

FLORENTINE ROLLS

2 pork fillets (50 dg each), 20 dg frozen spinach, 10 dg fresh cow cheese, 10 dg carrots, 2 cloves of garlic, 1 teaspoon Gussnela flour, 1 egg, salt, pepper, frying and roasting oil, 2 Vegeta tablespoons, Peel the skin from pork fillets, cut into lengthways, beat well with mallet to get bigger chops. Cook carrots and cut into strips, combine filtered spinach, fresh cow cheese, squeezed garlic, mixed egg, pepper and Vegeta. Arrange half the spinach and cheese mixture over the prepared steak, cover with cooked carrots and roll the steak. Fasten the ends with toothpicks and add sprinkle with some salt. Do the same with the other half. In oiled pan shortly fry prepared rolls. Then put them on greased tray, water, cover with alu foil and bake in the oven on 200°C for 50 minutes. When done, remove the toothpicks, cool and slice. Filter dripping, add flour previously mixed with water and cook shortly. Baste with dripping and serve with cooked potatoes.

Design
Gee + Chung

Art director, illustrator
Earl Gee

Designers
Earl Gee, Fani Chung

Printer
Digital Engraving

This company holiday party invitation had to link with Project READ, which promotes adult literacy, so Gee + Chung used a Christmas tree to represent the tree of knowledge. The die-cut tree on the card's front reveals a statement about literacy when it is removed, and the tree shape functions as a keepsake ornament or bookmark.

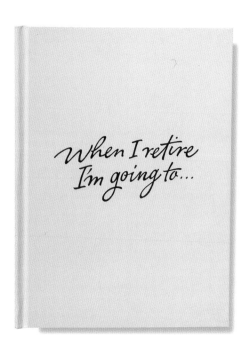

Design
Voice

Art directors, designers
Scott Carslake, Stuart Gluth

Paper artist
Stuart Gluth

Lettering
Don Hatcher

Printer
Regal Printing, Hong Kong

This extraordinary book was produced by Voice for its client, Map Financial Strategies, which develops financial solutions that meet particular investors' lifestyles. This design, created for the fifty-plus age demographic, tells a story of retirement. Using just die-cuts on all-white pages lets the viewer make the story his own, says designer Scott Carslake. He worked with a company that specializes in pop-up books and a talented paper artist to guarantee his idea's success. Grain direction and paper thickness definitely affect end results, he adds, so he advises working closely with the printer. A working dummy is a must.

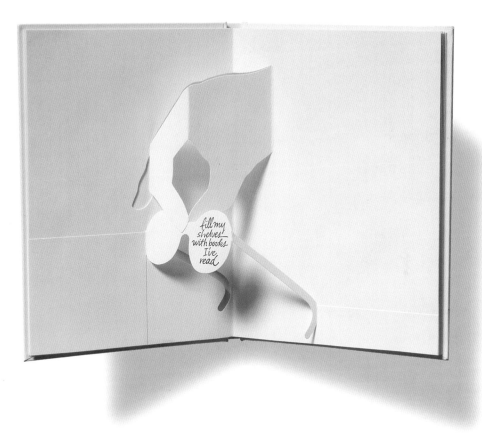

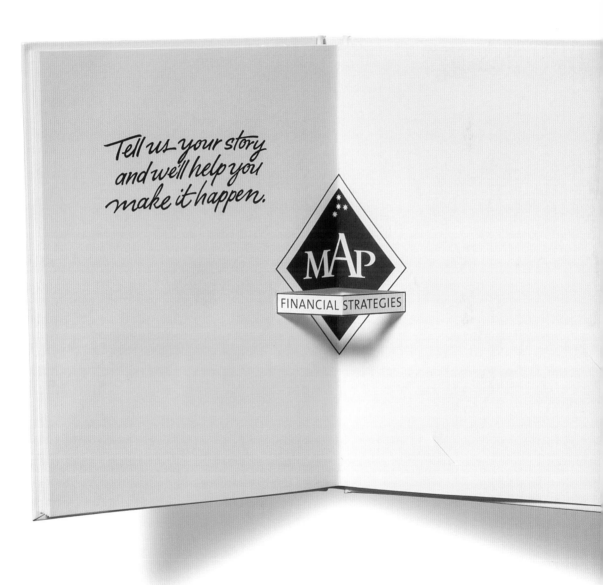

Intricate die cuts make this retirement planner
an attention-getting piece of work.

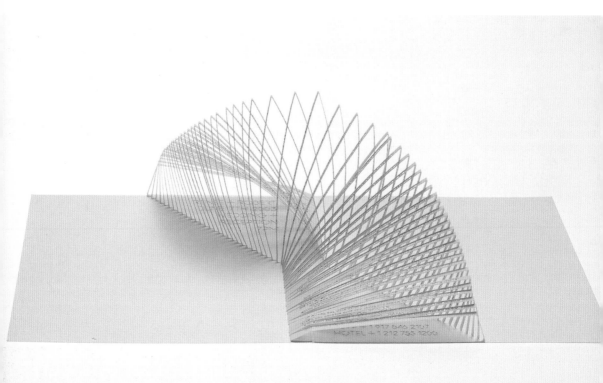

Design
Sagmeister, Inc., New York

Art director
Stefan Sagmeister

Designers
Stefan Sagmeister, Matthias
Ernstberger, Miso Wang

Manufacturer
Joe Freedman, Hestia
House/Sarabande Press

Created for close friends by
Stefan Sagmeister, this one-of-
a-kind invitation uses no
printing; it relies entirely on die-
cutting. Laser-cut onto 100
percent cotton paper selected
for its stability as well as its
wedding appropriateness, the
design's top, sliced layer tells the
story of how the couple met.
The base layer is the invitation
itself. Sagmeister says he
wanted the design to be
intricate and intriguing

Creative director

Billy Jurewicz

Associate creative director

Jason Strong

Designer

Benjamin Levitz, studio
ON FIRE

Production

Greg Krueger, AcuLine
& Metal Cards

Space150 redesigns its own
identity every 150 days, so its
designers have the opportunity
to learn plenty about specialty
production processes. Card
number sixteen is an aluminum
card, die-cut through stamping.
The copy was applied through
photochemical etching.

Chapter 6

Alternative Accents, Three-Dimensional Designs, and Add-ons: Spatial Relations and Fun

To design a three-dimensional piece, a designer has to think about spatial relations— a new sphere of consideration that has its own rules and constraints in terms of design, construction, scheduling, cost, production, and delivery. The recipient's reaction must be even more carefully considered: Will the extra effort and expense of building a dimensional piece harvest the proper amount of reaction or attention?

It is almost impossible to offer generic advice on how to create a three-dimensional design or add a three-dimensional accent to a two-dimensional design. Every design is utterly different. Each construction is a new feat of engineering. But the designers whose work is featured do offer some hard-won advice.

Concept is the most important factor to consider. The concept, as always, must meet the needs of the client, but the three-dimensional aspect or accent must also fit the equation as well. There has to be a very good reason for introducing a new dimension.

Building extra time in the schedule is critical. Producing a three-dimensional design or adding a three-dimensional element will add, at a minimum, five to ten days to any production schedule.

There are suppliers and even designers who specialize in pop-up design, such as printers that produce pop-up children's books. A quick review of the credits pages of books in the children's area of a larger bookstore will yield many resources.

Outside advice can also come from multidisciplinary design conferences; architects, product designers, and other professionals who work in three dimensions will be in attendance and can likely become resources.

Design Notes

> Produce plenty of mock-ups at final size to test the concept—a process that is time-consuming, says designer Nélida Nassar.

"We always build one-to-one prototypes of anything in three dimensions," says Stefan Sagmeister of Sagmeister, Inc. "Probably the most important ingredient is time management. Beside that, it is dummy building and dummy building and dummy building." Sagmeister also advises making friends with a product designer. "Then you have somebody to call on for manufacturing tips and three-dimensional rendering questions."

Another time-consuming aspect of such projects is that the designer often must rely on specialists from outside of the graphic design industry, such as structural engineers or even origami specialists, to develop a concept fully, adds Nélida Nassar. "Both the production and the manufacturing require more time, and budgets needed are also more expensive."

If you are specifying materials that regular or outside vendors usually do not work with—common with many three-dimensional designs—build even more time into the schedule, as they must have a learning curve to conquer as well. But even when a vendor is familiar with the materials that are specified, a particular graphic design may present different challenges from the ones they handle in their normal work.

Design Notes

> Designer Paul Sheriff wanted to stitch a cloth label—similar to a clothing label—onto the cover of a catalog. "It was a complicated task in that the label company is a leading vendor to the garment industry, and small orders are hard to come by. As for sewing the labels on the catalog, I researched companies that specialize in bookbinding but came across a company that does specialty banners," Sheriff says.

The full-size mock-up is a must, agrees Marcie Carson of IE Design + Communications. "Simple details are often overlooked when working on a flat digital file," she says, adding, "Allow time in the schedule to conduct a test mailing of the paper dummy that uses the exact paper stock, paper weight, folding, and so on."

Justin Ahrens of Rule29 builds comp after comp to figure out the best way to construct a design; then he speaks with his print and fabrication vendors to review the idea some more. "See if there is a better way to construct. Maybe a slight size change will make it print more economically," he says.

The materials that are selected are just as important. What type of paper will hold up best? Does it need to be scored so it doesn't crack? Will the finished design be durable enough to be enjoyed by the recipient?

To test durability and functionality, test dummies in the various environments in which the final needs to perform. How much does it cost to ship? Can it withstand shipping without being crushed or otherwise ruined? How simple is it to store — both before and after distribution? Can the recipient figure it out? In some cases, if the design will take the recipient too long to assemble or manipulate, it won't be used at all.

Keeping costs down can be a challenge. Whether the cause is the extra time such a project requires, materials, or manufacturing, three-dimensional designs cost more. Be willing to compromise a bit —say, on paper stock or size—when necessary, if it doesn't affect the final outcome too much. Also, on shorter runs, consider keeping final production aspects or mailing in-house.

Once the final design is ready to print, get as many drawdowns, test die samples, scoring, and other trials as possible from the printer or production house. The more complex the piece, the more issues must be settled before the job is printed.

The most common advice from designers is pessimistic but practical: Double the budget and double the time. But they also add this: When concept and dimension are well married, the outcome is often well worth the effort.

MORE ABOUT

Drawdowns

A drawdown is a smear or stroke of ink made on the sheet of paper or other substrate to be used in a print order, produced so colors and substrate performance can be checked prior to printing.

Scoring

A score is a crease that is applied, through a scoring die or line strike on press, to a sheet of paper so it is easier to fold in that spot. Scoring is especially important on heavier paper stocks or when a fold must be made against the grain of a paper. It prevents the paper from looking ragged on the folding edge and maintains the paper's surface. On a single job, scores may be made that help paper fold up or down.

Design
Schwadesign

"Schwadesign.com is now refreshed." So reads the back of this lenticular postcard, designed to demonstrate in a visual and dynamic way the notion of refreshed interactivity. Schwadesign's "minister of perspective" Josh Silverman says setting up files for lenticular surfaces is simple: "Set up layered Illustrator files in the order you'd like them to appear, designating each stage of the image along the way. The printer takes care of the rest."

Design
Orlando Facioli Design

Client
Mario Queiroz Fashion Show

This invitation to a fashion show was designed to reflect the show's pop art theme; in fact, designer Orlando Facioli wanted the design to look like a piece of pop art. He printed on silicon sheets for the envelope and used holographic plastic for the inside. The rubbery outside envelope deadens the high coloration of the inside piece, but once the insert is removed, its colors shift and change.

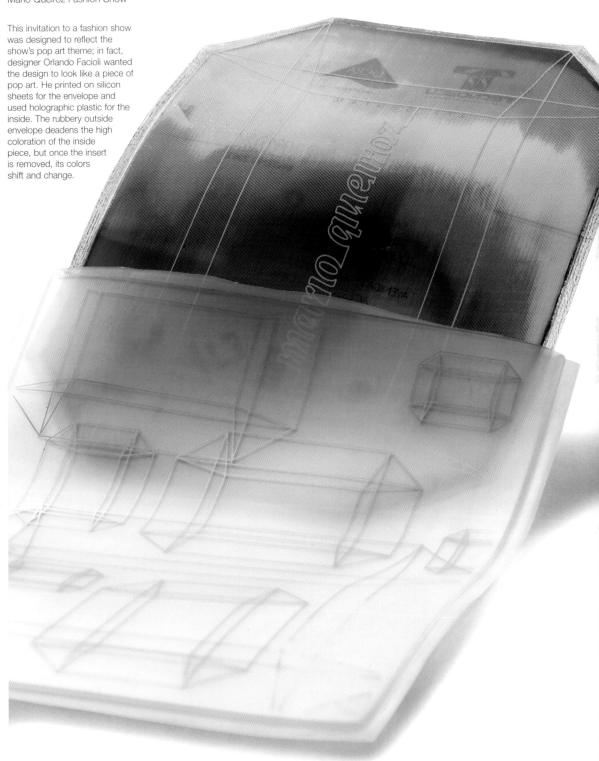

Design
IE Design + Communications

Creative director
Marcie Carson

Art director, designer
Jane Lee

Printers
Roadrunner Press, Donahue
Printing

Client
Kai's Catering

A second color was added to
this simple invitation with thread,
added with a standard sewing
machine. The waved lines
represented the beachfront
location of the wedding.

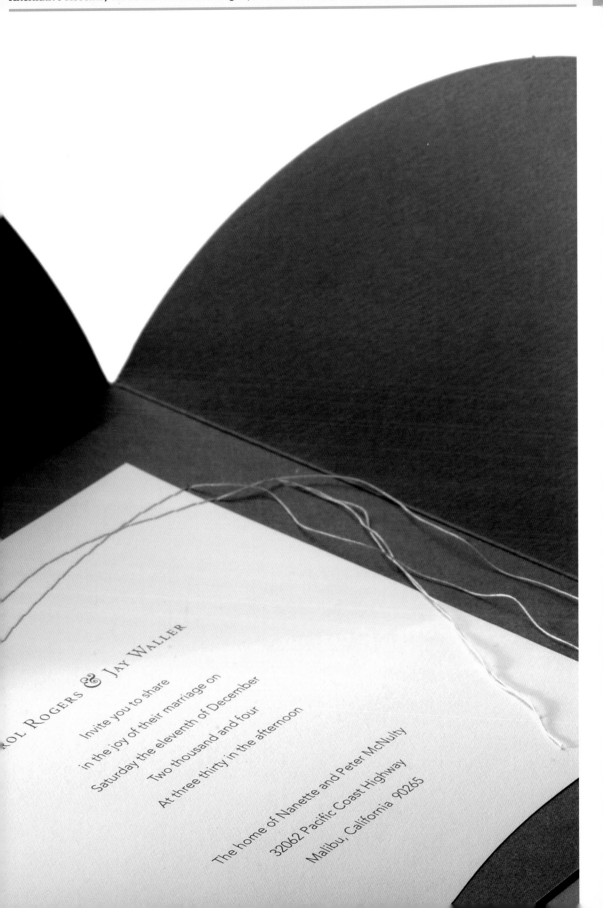

ROL ROGERS & JAY WALLER

Invite you to share

in the joy of their marriage on

Saturday the eleventh of December

Two thousand and four

At three thirty in the afternoon

The home of Nanette and Peter McNulty

32062 Pacific Coast Highway

Malibu, California 90265

Design
Paul Sheriff Design

This sewn museum show
catalog cover adds a surprise
design element—a cloth tag that
carries the title of the show. The
tags were produced by a
garment industry vendor.
Securing such a small order was
difficult, says designer Paul
Sheriff. Another concern was
specifying a paper tough
enough to withstand a double
line stitched across the front and
back of the book without
perforating and weakening it.

Design
John Kneapler Design

Art director
John Kneapler

Designers
John Kneapler, Colleen Shea,
Niccole White

Printer
Intographics NYC

For the James Beard
Foundation, a nonprofit culinary
and cooking organization, John
Kneapler Design created an
invitation for the group's annual
fund-raising gala. After
researching the idea of
connecting some sort of spice
to the card—a unique visual
with tactile and aromatic
qualities—the designers chose
cinnamon sticks because they
are economical, graphically
pleasing, and durable. Selecting
the right envelope was crucial,
says principal John Kneapler, to
make sure the sticks would not
be crushed when mailed.

Design
Sussner Design Co.

Designer
Brandon Van Liere

Art director
Derek Sussner

Copywriters
Steve Seidl, Judy Kirk

Photographer
Gary Woodward

Printer
Reflections

Client
Target Commercial Interiors

For the VIP grand opening invitation for Target Commercial Interiors, Sussner Design Company used a real piece of red carpet onto which they adhered the invite copy. The carpet not only played off the VIP red carpet treatment idea but also the color of the Target brand. For a later brochure, the designers used the same approach.

Design
Zoe Scutts Design

Production
Stuart O'Neill

Printer
Richard Murray

Plastic Case
Anton Clemens

Client
Nick Veasey

To celebrate a decade of his X-ray photography, Nick Veasey produced a miniportfolio that mimicked his actual one. On the side of the injection-molded minicase, pressed into the plastic, is the artist's Web address. Inside is a tiny perfect-bound book that displays his work. Veasey's advice on such projects: "Double the budget, double the time scale."

Design
Nassar Design

Creative director
Nélida Nassar

Designers
Nélida Nassar, Margarita
Encomienda

Copywriter
Raymonde Abou

Printer
Anis Commercial Printing
Press

Client
Collége Louise Wegmann

This school fund-raising
brochure contains three simple
but elegant pop-ups, each
representing a different level of
donation option. The staggered
and die-cut folder edge is a
memorable and gentle approach
to involving recipients in giving to
the school.

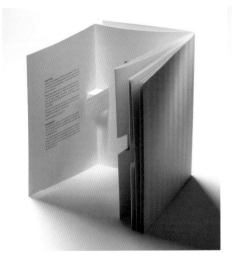

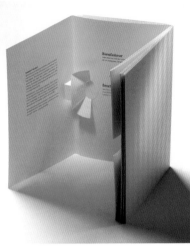

Design
IE Design + Communications

Creative director
Marcie Carson

Art director
Jane Lee

Client
ISC Viterbi School of
Engineering

Here's a pop-up that grabs the recipient's attention—crucial, as the recipient is likely to be a college-bound student already inundated with recruitment literature. Appropriately, this highly engineered piece was created for a school of engineering. A miniposter emerges from what appears to be an innocuous self-mailer.

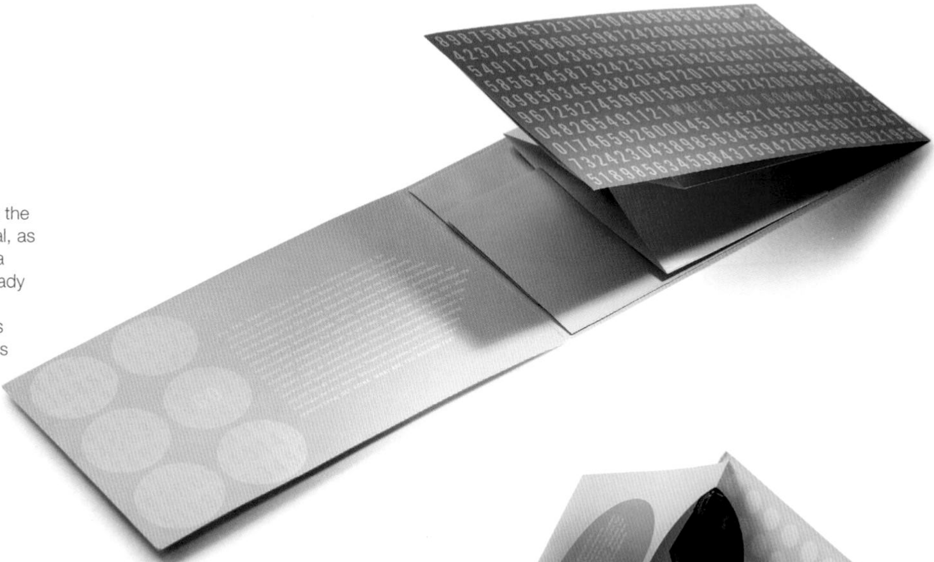

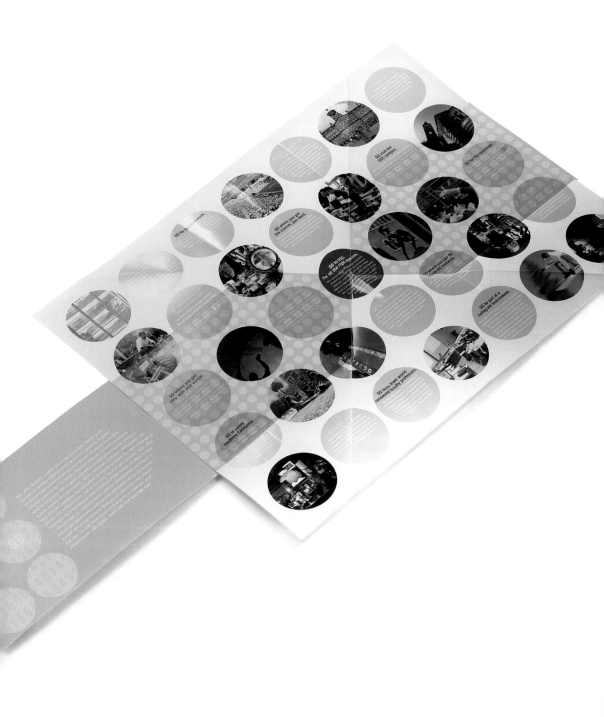

Design
Sagmeister Inc., New York

Art direction
Stefan Sagmeister

Designers
Matthias Ernstberger, Sarah Noellenheidt

Client
Sagmeister, Inc.

These business cards aren't cheap; in fact, at 90 cents (£ .47) a unit, they are mighty precious. But they are also incredibly memorable and speak loudly of the dramatic work from Sagmeister, Inc. The design is offset printed, then laser-cut and hand-assembled. Interns were integral to the process, Sagmeister says.

Design
m-Art

Calligraphy
Takeo Ichimura

Painting
Kaii Higashiyama

Client
The Washington Opera

A-list Washington receives many invitations to black-tie galas, so designer Marty Ittner of m-Art wanted to find a special way to attract this audience's attention for an Opera Ball at the Japanese Embassy. The solution is an invitation secreted inside a fan. It carries a tritone of a Japanese painting, a foil stamp, embossed calligraphy and a silk tassel.

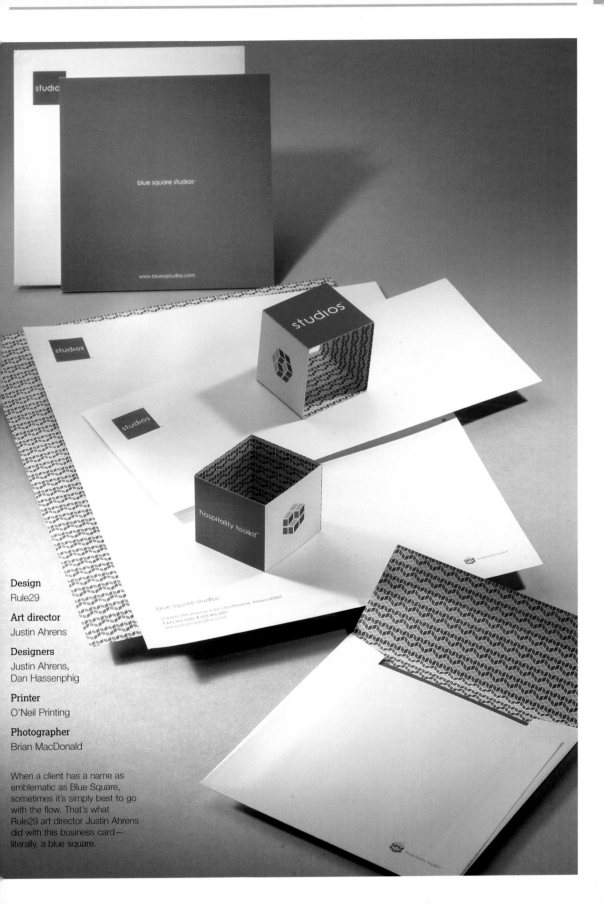

Design
Rule29

Art director
Justin Ahrens

Designers
Justin Ahrens,
Dan Hassenphig

Printer
O'Neil Printing

Photographer
Brian MacDonald

When a client has a name as
emblematic as Blue Square,
sometimes it's simply best to go
with the flow. That's what
Rule29 art director Justin Ahrens
did with this business card—
literally, a blue square.

Design

Renee Rech Design

Designers

Renee Rech, Semra Erden

Client

Atlas Peak, Beam Wine Estates

The client for this project, a winery, requested that a piece be designed in a triangular shape that would pop up to a pyramid or peak matching the company's logo. A consistent brand message was crucial for its line of premier mountain cabernets. Renee Rech and Semra Erden created a design with two purposes: Flat, it served as a regular brochure; assembled, it turned into a dimensional display piece showcasing the client's cabernets. Because folds went in many directions, proper paper selection was crucial, says Rech.

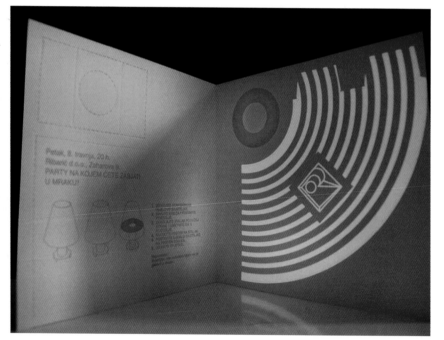

Design
Bruketa&Zinic

Art director
Ana Belic

Creative director
Tonka Lujanac

Designer
Luka Juras

Copywriter
Daniel Vukovic

Client
Ribaric

Requiring the recipient of a design to assemble it into its final form involves that person far more than a flat mailer does. This invitation, designed by Bruketa&Zinic, was produced for the opening of a new office for a lighting company. The sample light, printed with glow-in-the-dark ink, makes a simple but memorable statement.

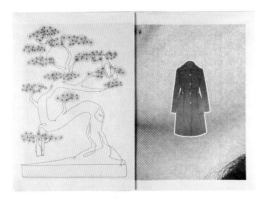

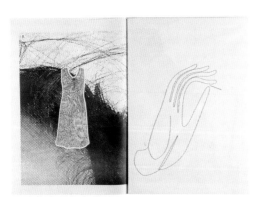

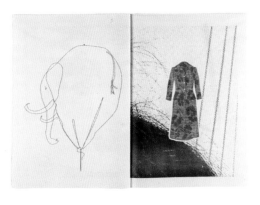

Design
Sagmeister Inc., New York

Art director
Stefan Sagmeister

Illustrator, photographer, designer
Richard The

Client
Anni Kuan

What starts as a series of flat promotional pieces—32 pages printed on affordable newsprint—becomes something else entirely when it is reassembled by the recipient, using pins supplied with the fashion catalog.

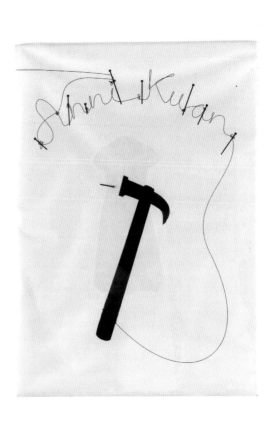

Design
Lloyds Graphic Design Ltd.

Concept, art director, designer, photographer
Alexander Lloyd

Printing
Blenheim Printing Company Ltd.

Box
Berica Marketing

Screenprinting, patches
Newman Graphics

Shirts
The Warehouse

This self-promotion was based around the concept of a design studio being akin to an auto repair shop: providing solid traditional work and good value. An assembled piece with many components is expensive, reports designer Alexander Lloyd. This one contains a booklet, swing tags, product wraps, labels, a notebook, screenprinted shirt, and an embroidered patch. But the promo was exceptionally well received by clients and associates alike, says Lloyd— well worth the extra effort.

Design
Lloyds Graphic Design Ltd.

Art director, designer
Alexander Lloyd

Printing
Blenheim Printing Company Ltd.

Box, mints
Berica Marketing

Pen radio, tin
Signature Promotions

Clips
Corporate Express

Another multipiece annual promotion from Lloyds Graphic Design. Pulling such designs together requires careful orchestration of supplies from many sources—as well as plenty of time, says principal Alexander Lloyd. This designer spy kit pulls together a host of goodies, including mints, pen radio, secret files, and much more. It's crucial with these multipiece designs, says Lloyd, to be ready to adapt your concept or elements of it when time frames or production limitations dictate. "Sometimes the ability to compromise can be the key to avoiding unnecessary grief or stress," he says.

Design

Spiral Design

Design team

Robert Clancy, Lauren Payne,
Neil Wright, Jeanie Guity,
Maureen Mooney, Anne
Hobday, Emily Rawitsch,
Gina Krajca, Bryan Kowalski

Mechanics, engineering

Ken Gasch, HLD Productions

The Spiralizer is an extravaganza of three-dimensional design, so much so that the unique holiday gift is actually an entirely new product, hand-built and filled with hand-assembled machinery. The fortune-telling device arrives with a letter that speaks of its mysterious origins and enchanting powers. Its creators wanted the gift to tell clients and peers about the design studio's passion for collaborative teamwork, creativity, and fun. Every member of the Spiral Design team worked on the promotion.

Designer, photographer

Jimmy Ball

Printer

Jay Kay Press

Client

Ethan Sloan

Designer Jimmy Ball wanted to produce something extra special to announce the birth of his son. He gave the standard new-dad cigar a new twist: A brown leatherette paper backs the actual announcement—printed with an ashlike pattern on its back—and everything is rolled and secured with a baby-blue cigar band/ribbon. An extra tail of brown paper sticks out of the rolled design and is twisted to enhance the cigar illusion.

Suppliers

An exhaustive list of all of the organizations that supply the printing effects and materials discussed in this book would be impossible to compile. Instead, the following resource list should give the designer plenty of knowledgeable sources from which to assemble information that is specific to projects and locations.

Binding

Binding Industries Association
200 Deer Run Road
Sewickley, PA 15143
412.741.6860
412.741.2311 fax
www.gain.net

Die-Cutting

**International Association of
Diecutting and Diemaking (IADD)**
651 W. Terra Cotta Avenue, Suite 132
Crystal Lake, IL 60014
815.455.7519
815.455.7510 fax

Embossing/Debossing

**Foil Stamping and Embossing
Association (FSEA)**
2150 SW Westport Drive, Suite 101
Topeka, KS 66614
785.271.5816
785.271.6404 fax
www.fsea.com

Foil Printing/Stamping

Association of Hot Foil Printers
15 Hunt Street
Atherton, Manchester
M46 9JF UK
01942 873574
0845 166 8396 fax
www.hotfoilprinting.org

**Foil Stamping and Embossing
Association (FSEA)**
2150 SW Westport Drive, Suite 101
Topeka, KS 66614
785.271.5816
785.271.6404 fax
www.fsea.com

Letterpress

Amalgamated Printers Association
www.apa-letterpress.org

**The Association of Handcraft
Printers (NZ) (AHP)**
124 Richardson Road
Owairaka, Auckland 1003
New Zealand
www.letterpress.org.nz
(General information on letterpress)
www.letterpress.ch
www.fiveroses.org/intro.htm
(Directory of letterpress printers)
www.briarpress.org
(Monthly newspaper about letterpress)

Letterpress Green Sheet
PO Box 671
Ada, MI 49301
SpeedGray@aol.com

Letterpress Printers of the World
www.letterpressprinters.org
  /bios_004.htm

Paper
(Directory of handmade and high-quality
papers)

Briar Press
www.briarpress.org

Grade Finders
662 Exton Commons
Exton, PA 19341
610.524.7070
610.524.8912 fax
www.npes.org

PaperAge magazine
185 Lincoln Street, Suite 200B
Hingham, MA 02043
781.749.5255
781.749.5896 fax

Printing, General

British Printing Society (BPS)
www.bpsnet.org.uk

China Dyeing and Printing Association
www.cdpa.org.cn

Graphic Arts Association
1210 Northbrook Drive, Suite 250
Trevose, PA 19053
215.396.2300
215.396.9890 fax
www.gaa.com

Graphic Arts Association of Hong Kong (GAAHK)
13G World Tech Centre
95 How Ming Street
Kwun Tong KLN, Hong Kong
2856.9760
2856.9765 fax
www.gaahk.org

Graphic Professionals Resource Network
7042 Brooklyn Boulevard
Minneapolis, MN 55429
800.466.4274
763.560.1350 fax
www.iaphc.org

Ink World magazine
20 Dunton Avenue
Deer Park, NY 11729
631.586.3666
631.586.3874 fax

National Association of Printing Ink Manufacturers (NAPIM)
581 Main Street
Woodbridge, NJ 07095
732.855.1525
732.855.1838 fax
www.napim.org

Printing Industries of America/Graphic Arts Technical Foundation (PIA/GATF)
200 Deer Run Road
Sewickley, PA 15143
412.741.6860
412.741.2311 fax
www.gain.net

Printing Industry Association of Australia
25 South Parade
Aubern NSW 2144
02.8789.7300
02.8789.7387 fax
www.printnet.com.au

Thai Printing Association
www.thaiprint.org

Waterless Printing Association (WPA)
PO Box 1252
Woodstock, IL 60098
815.337.7681
815.337.7682 fax
www.waterless.org

Screenprinting

Digital and Screen Printing Association (DSPA)
Association House
7a West Street
Reigate, Surrey
RH2 9BL UK
www.spauk.co.uk

Specialty Printing/Inks

International Ink Company
775 Dorsey Street
Gainesville, GA 30501
770.531.0033
770.531.0099 fax
www.iicink.com

Specialty Graphic Imaging Association (SGIA)
10015 Main Street
Fairfax, VA 22031
703.385.1335
703.273.0456 fax
www.sgia.org

Specialty Ink Company
20 Dunton Avenue
Deer Park, NY 11729
800.253.3840
631.586.3874 fax
www.specialtyink.com

Thermography

Worldwide Printing Thermographers Association
305 Plus Park Boulevard
Nashville, TN 37217
800.821.3138
615.366.4192 fax
www.thermographers.org

Contributors

Kevin Akers Design + Imagery
4095 Lilac Ridge Road
San Ramon, CA 94583
925.735.1015
www.kevinakers.com
page 25

And Partners
158 W. Twenty-Seventh Street,
Floor 7
New York, NY 10001
212.414.4700
www.andpartnersny.com
page 90

Jimmy Ball Design
972.333.7251
page 159

Blockdot
8350 N. Central Expressway,
Suite 400
Dallas, TX 75206
214.890.4100
www.blockdot.com
pages 30–31

**Be a Design Group/Bennett
Holzworth**
831 Williams Avenue
Hastings, NE 68901
402.463.5544
www.bennettholzworth.com
www.beadesigngroup.com
page 23

Blok Design
Sombrerete 515, No. 1
La Condesa, Mexico DF 06170
Mexico City, Mexico
55.15.2423
page 92

Boccalatte
PO Box 370
Surry Hills 2010
Sydney, NSW Australia
612.9310.4149
www.boccalatte.com
page 65

Blu Concept, Inc.
103-1104-1104 Hornby Street
Vancouver, BC
V6Z W8 Canada
604.872.2583
www.bluconcept.com
pages 44, 91, 96

Bruketa&Zinic
Zavrtnica 17
Zagreb, 10 000
Croatia
385.16.064.000
www.bruketa-zinic.com
pages 94–95, 114–115,
118–121, 152–153

**Creative Consumer
Concepts–C3**
10955 Granada Lane
Overland Park, KS 66211
913.327.2241
www.c3.to
pages 29, 38

Citizen Scholar
303 Park Avenue S., #1005
New York, NY 10010
646.797.3319
www.citizenscholar.com
page 72

Dave Clark Design
1305 E. Fifteenth Street, Suite 202
Tulsa, OK 74120
918.295.0044
page 81

Orlando Facioli
Rua São Carlos do Pinhai 152/92
São Paolo SP 01333-000
Brazil
www.orlandofacioli.com.br
pages 26–27, 74, 135

Form
47 Tabernacle Street
London EC22 4AA UK
20 7014 1430
www.form.uk.com
page 60–61, 116

Fossil
972.234.2525
www.fossil.com
pages 32–35

**Full Circle Marketing and
Design**
1324 Lake Drive SE, Suite 6
Grand Rapids, MI 49506
616.915.1951
www.thinkfullcircle.com
page 71

Gee + Chung Design
38 Bryant Street, Suite 100
San Francisco, CA 94105
415.543.1192
www.geechungdesign.com
pages 24, 110–111, 122–123

Grapevine
105 N. Street
Boston, MA 02127
617.268.9409
www.grapevinepaperie.com
pages 37, 41, 98

Hollis Brand Communications
680 W. Beech Street, Suite 1
San Diego, CA 92101
619.234.2061
pages 64, 73

Ruth Huimerind
Rännaku Pst. 9-29
10917 Tallinn
Estonia
372.51.11501
www.hot.ee/rosapermante
pages 62–63, 109

Hutchinson Associates, Inc.
1147 W. Ohio Street
Chicago, IL 60622
312.455.9191
www.hutchinson.com
pages 79, 112

Iggesund Paperboard, Inc.
1050 Wall Street W. Suite 640
Lyndhurst, NJ 07071
201.804.9977
www.iggesundpaperboard.com
page 57

IE Design + Communications
422 Pacific Coast Highway
Hermosa Beach, CA 90254
310.376.9600
www.iedesign.net
pages 113, 136–137, 144–145

Tomato Kosir s.p.
Britof 141
Kranj, Slovenia
SI-4000 Slovenia-EU
386.41.260.979
www.tomatokosir.com
pages 55, 76–77

Peter Kruty Editions
365 Fortieth Street
Brooklyn, NY 11232
718.788.1542
www.peterkrutyeditions.com
pages 36, 82–83

Kinetic
2 Leng Kee Road
Thye Hong Centre, #04-03A
Hong Kong
65.63795792
page 117

John Kneapler Design
151 W. Nineteenth Street, Suite 11C
New York, NY 10011
212.463.9774
www.johnkneaplerdesign.com
page 139

**Licher Art &
Design/Independent
Project Press**
45 Castle Rock Road, Suite 3
Sedona, AZ 86351
928.284.1282
land@esedona.net
pages 99–101

Lloyds Graphic Design Ltd.
Studio One Seven
17 Westhaven Place
Blenheim, New Zealand
64 3 578 6955
pages 156–157

Lubell, Brodsky, Inc.
158 Linwood Plaza, Suite 227
Fort Lee, NJ 07024
917.716.8181
ed@edbrodsky.com
page 21

m-Art
7902 Flower Avenue
Takoma Park, MD 20912
301.588.8591
www.m-art.org
Nassar Design
11 Park Street
Brookline, MA 02446
617.264.2862
page 148

Michael Osborne Design
444 De Haro, Suite 207
San Francisco, CA 94107
415.255.0125
www.modsf.com
pages 80, 93

Nassar Design
11 Park Street
Brookline, MA 02446
617.264.2862
pages 20, 56, 143

Oxide Design
4013 Farnam Street
Omaha, NE 68131
402.344.0168
www.oxidedesign.com
pages 42–43

Pensaré Design Group
1313 F Street NW
Washington, DC 20004
202.638.7700
www.pensaredesign.com
page 75

Sigi Ramoser
Sägenvier DesignKomminikation
Sägerstrasse 4, A-6850
Dornbirn, Austria
0043.650.2748100
www.saegenvier.at
page 28

Renee Rech Design
415.775.9521
www.reneerechdesign.com
pages 52–53, 150–151

Red Canoe
347 Clear Creek Trail
Deer Lodge, TN 37726
423.965.2223
www.redcanoe.com
page 78

Refinery Design Company
2001 Alta Vista Street
Dubuque, IA 52001
563.584.0172
page 39

Rule29
303 W. State Street
Geneva, IL 60134
630.262.1009
www.rule29.com
pages 55, 149

Sagmeister Inc.
222 W. Fourteenth Street, Apt. 15A
New York, NY 10011
212.647.1789
pages 128, 146–147, 154–155

Schwadesign
560 Mineral Spring Avenue,
Studio 202
Pawtucket, RI 02860
617.912.9434
page 134

Paul Sheriff Design
page 138

Space150
212 Third Avenue N.
Suite 150
Minneapolis, MN 55401
612.332.6458
www.space150.com
page 129

Spiral Design Studio
915 Broadway
Albany, NY 12207
518.432.7976
www.spiraldesign.com
pages 97, 158

Stereobloc
Albrecht und Stumpe GbR
Linienstrabe 214
10119 Berlin, Germany
49.30.447310.13
www.stereobloc.de
page 54

Sussner Design Co.
212 Third Avenue N.
Minneapolis, MN 55401
612.339.3886
www.sussner.com
pages 58–59, 140–141

Underware
Amsterdam, Den Haag, Helsinki
31.20.52.89.770
www.underware.nl
page 22

Nick Veasey/Radar Studio
Coldblow Lane
Thurnham Maidstone, Kent
ME14 3LR UK
44.1622.737722
www.nickveasey.com
page 142

Voice
217 Gilbert Street
Adelaide, SA 5000
Australia
618.8410.8822
www.voicedesign.net
pages 124–125

Vrontikis Design Office
2707 Westwood Boulevard
Los Angeles, CA 90064
310.446.5446
www.35k.com
page 45

Index

About the Author

Graphic design and illustration have been the focus for writer and editor **Catharine Fishel** for more than two decades. She is a contributing editor to *Print* magazine, editor of LogoLounge.com, and author of many books on the subject of design.

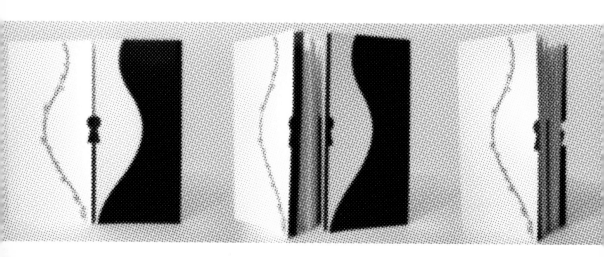